VISIONS

OF THE

HARVEST

25th Anniversary Edition

RICK JOYNER

MorningStar Publications

A DIVISION OF MORNINGSTAR FELLOWSHIP CHURCH

375 Star Light Drive, Fort Mill, SC 29715

www.MorningStarMinistries.org

Visions of the Harvest
by Rick Joyner
Copyright © 1998
25th Anniversary Edition, 2012

Distributed by MorningStar Publications, Inc.,
a division of MorningStar Fellowship Church,
375 Star Light Drive, Fort Mill, SC 29715
www.MorningStarMinistries.org

International Standard Book Number—1-60708-434-1; 978-1-60708-434-1

Unless otherwise indicated, all Scripture quotations are taken from the
New American Standard Bible, copyright © 1960, 1962, 1963, 1968, 1971,
1973, 1974, 1977 by The Lockman Foundation. Italics in Scripture are for
emphasis only.

Table of Contents

A Vision of the Harvest..5

   Chapter One
   The Final Clash of Light and Darkness........................ 11

   Chapter Two
   The Fishnet.. 21

   Chapter Three
   Tribulation and Glory 27

   Chapter Four
   Exhortations From the Throne.................................... 31

The Titanic and the Stock Market 39

   Chapter One
   Foundations Are Important 41

War and Glory 91

The Next Wave Is Upon Us 115

Catching the Next Wave 123

A VISION OF THE HARVEST

In 1987, I had a two-and-a-half-day prophetic experience in which I was shown two great worldwide moves of God like waves that would come upon the earth. Both of these would eclipse every previous revival in history. The first would be so great that much of the body of Christ would think that it was the harvest that Jesus said would be the end of this age. It was not, but it was the ingathering of those who were called to be laborers in the greatest harvest and the greatest move of God of all-time that would come after it.

The first wave that I was shown began just a couple of years after I had this experience. Over the following twelve to sixteen years, more people came to Christ around the world than had come to Him through the entire church age before that time. At the peak of this move, it was estimated that nearly four hundred thousand new believers were coming in every day worldwide. Nothing had ever been seen like this before. Some of the greatest evangelists and missionaries in history were released during this time, and whole nations were transformed. It is understandable that many thought this was the harvest that would be the end of this age. It was not. A much bigger wave will soon break upon the world.

In the 1987 experience, I was shown that between these two great waves of harvest there would be a period of relative spiritual quiet. I was not shown how long this would last, but that we would need all of this time to get ready for the great move of God that is coming, which will be the greatest move of God to ever come upon the earth. We have been in this period for about a decade now. In 2011, I was shown that we do not have much more time before the next great wave will break upon the earth. The messages in this book can help us get ready.

All of these messages came in 1987 and the next few years after it. They have been published and widely distributed before, but this is an updated version, which includes all of the understanding I've gained in the last twenty-five years about the greatest of all events to come upon the world. This is the time that the prophets and righteous of old desired to see and that we have been chosen to live in. There has never been a greater time to know and walk with God than the time that we are about to enter. There is a lot of work to do, but the power of the Lord will be with us. It is now time to give our top priority to getting ready.

The major factors in the coming move of God will be the following:

1. the unprecedented ingathering of new believers,

2. the preaching of the gospel of the kingdom throughout the earth,

3. the church becoming the "holy nation" it is called to be, a kingdom culture that spreads throughout the earth,

4. the emergence of apostolic and prophetic authority that measure up to their biblical stature,

5. the forming of councils of apostles and elders to govern the "holy nation" with divine wisdom and grace,

6. all other authority on earth that is not obedient to the Lord will continue to collapse,

7. and the church, "the bride of Christ," will make herself ready, becoming the greatest demonstration of God's love, and the power of that love, since Jesus walked the earth.

The following is written to help us get ready by understanding the times, the unfolding events, and to see the coming kingdom so that we can help prepare the way for the coming King.

Chapter One
THE FINAL CLASH OF LIGHT AND DARKNESS

A harvest is coming greater than all that came before it. In Matthew 13:39, Jesus stated that **"the harvest is the end of the age,"** and at the end of this age the earth will experience the greatest ingathering of believers into Christ than in all other previous moves of God combined. Over and over Jesus warned that laborers were needed for the harvest, and this is one of the most desperate needs of the hour. This is not just for evangelists to reap the harvest, but for pastors and teachers to get them healed, delivered, and established on sound biblical doctrine, and then for prophets and apostles to help build them into the "city set on a hill" that the church is called to be.

Because the harvest is the reaping of what has been sown, both the good and bad that has been sown in man will be coming to full maturity together. Isaiah 60:1-2 described this time:

> **"Arise, shine; for your light has come, and the glory of the LORD has risen upon you.**

> **"For behold, darkness will cover the earth, and deep darkness the peoples; but the LORD will rise upon you, and His glory will appear upon you."**

As we see here, it is at the very time that darkness is covering the earth and deep darkness the people that the glory of the Lord is appearing on His people. This time will be the ultimate clash between light and darkness, and both will be in their full maturity. Even so, the next three verses in this prophecy declare the outcome (see Isaiah 60:3-5):

> **"Nations will come to your light, and kings to the brightness of your rising.**

> **"Lift up your eyes round about, and see; they all gather together, they come to you. Your sons will come from afar, and your daughters will be carried in the arms.**

> **"Then you will see and be radiant, and your heart will thrill and rejoice; because the abundance of the sea will be turned to you, the wealth of the nations will come to you."**

This is the "sure word of prophecy" that cannot fail. The light wins! The nations may be led astray by the darkness for a time, but ultimately they will turn to the light and the glory that is appearing on God's people. A victory can only be as big as the battle, and this will be the ultimate battle and the ultimate victory. Losing is not an option, and it is not a fair fight—our God is all-powerful and He will triumph. His Word will come to pass.

Mature Mantles

We must keep this in mind through the times ahead because there may be times when it seems victory is impossible and that evil is prevailing. It will not stand. What the Lord is about to release on the earth will be like thousands of John the Baptists, thousands like the Apostle Paul, thousands like Luther, Calvin, Zwingli, Zinzendorf, Wesley, Whitefield, Edwards, Elliot, Fenny, and others, many of which are already serving and reaping a great harvest.

At the end of this age, a mature spirit of Elijah anointing will be coming upon a great number of prophets. This anointing will be imparted to the whole church for the fulfilling of the last two verses in the Old Testament, Malachi 4:5-6:

"Behold, I am going to send you Elijah the prophet before the coming of the great and terrible day of the LORD.

"He will restore the hearts of the fathers to *their* children, and the hearts of the children to their fathers, lest I come and smite the land with a curse."

This is essential for the glory of the Lord to be revealed by His people. Honoring our fathers and mothers is the only commandment with a promise and is included in both the Old and New Testaments. The promise is stated in Ephesians 6:2-3:

Honor your father and mother (which is the first commandment with a promise),

so that it may be well with you, and that you may live long on the earth.

Of course, this commandment has to do with our natural parents. It has been through the dishonoring of parents, especially fathers and fatherhood, that a major gate of hell has been opened upon the earth, which creates much of the darkness and lawlessness that is emerging in these times. However, this is not just about our natural parents, but it is for our spiritual parents as well. We honor our parents by remembering them and heeding their teaching. Many Christians are going to discover the deep wells of wisdom and knowledge by the great spiritual fathers and mothers in history. By drinking from the wells that they dug, they will receive an anointing, and in some cases, their mantle.

14

The Holy Spirit is the Helper, not the Doer. He does not come upon us and use us like robots, but He helps us with our commission. The Lord loves the diversity of His creation, and when His Spirit comes upon us, it does not make us into robots, but unites with who we are. This is why John the Baptist, who came in the spirit of Elijah, was very different from Elijah in many ways. Elijah walked in extraordinary supernatural power, but John the Baptist did not—he was more a preacher of righteousness. Authentic ministries are never copies of the originals, but all are unique just as we see everyone in Scripture being unique.

We also must keep in mind that we are seeking to grow up into Christ, not just be one of His messengers. Even so, there are mantles or anointings that are passed down, even though they may manifest differently with each one who receives them. Just as the Lord's garments were divided after His crucifixion, mantles also are usually divided and part of them given to many, not just one. They also mature with each one who wears them. At the end of this age, they will be fully mature and more powerful than ever.

While it is always right to honor those who have gone before us to prepare the way for what we are now walking in, we must combine this respect with knowledge that we also have our own destiny. We are not trying to create the first century church, but the twenty-first century church. We should love, honor, and receive all that we can from the great vessels in history, but we cannot fulfill our own purpose by trying to be like them. We must be who God created us to be.

One of the ultimate conflicts between the light and darkness at the end of this age will be between the controlling, dominating, totalitarian spirit that seeks to destroy the human spirit by making people automatons. The Holy Spirit has come to set us free to be who God created us to be and who can worship Him in Spirit and in truth from our hearts. The bold, confident, uniqueness of Christians at the end of this age will be a manifestation of His glory, which will stand out as brilliant beacons to those who have had their humanity stolen by the totalitarian spirit of the age.

David could not wear Saul's armor to fight the enemy the way he was skilled at fighting. It was an honorable thing for Saul to offer David his own armor, and David honored Saul by trying to wear it, but he also needed to have the wisdom and resolution to take it off. We will not be able to accomplish our purpose in our generation by doing things the way the last generation did them. We need to honorably reject many of the ways of our spiritual fathers and mothers. The key word here is "honorably," but we must do it.

What is still today called "modern missions" actually began with Zinzendorf and the Moravians more than two hundred and fifty years ago. The mission strategies of those times were developed to take advantage of the travel and communications of the times, but are far out of step with our own times. Some of the most powerful messengers and missionaries of these times could be bloggers or video producers. The pulpits of our time are television and the Internet more than the traditional podium. The Moravians could take six months to get to a mission post, when there is virtually no place on earth today that cannot be reached in six days or less.

It is time to put off Saul's armor, which may have worked well for him, but is far out of step with these times. Even so, the message must not change, but in fact, in many ways, it has been changed. The original must be recovered if we are going to accomplish our purpose. The gospel of the kingdom, which is the gospel of Jesus Christ, who He is and where He now sits, the purpose and power of His cross, and the power of His resurrection, must be recovered and preached throughout the world.

The "last trumpet" in the Book of Revelation, or the last message of this age, is that "our God reigns." If there is any change to the presentation of the gospel, we will see it change from "Come to Him" to "Bow the knee! He is the ruler of heaven and earth."

This is not to imply that the gospel of salvation, which we have redemption and salvation only through the cross of Jesus, will ever change. Even so, in this age it was an invitation to come to Him. In Revelation 3:20, we even see Him standing outside the door of His own church to see if any will open to Him. This is because this whole age since His resurrection has been for the calling and preparation of those who would rule with Him in the age to come. As we come to the end of this age, the message will change from this invitation to "He reigns."

Even though the message will change in this way, it is good news, not bad. As the times unfold, all of heaven and earth will witness the maturity of rebellion, the consequences of mankind trying to rule without walking with God. The lesson will be so complete that no being in all of creation will want to ever try that again. When the world starts to hear that the Lord is coming to take His rightful place, that His kingdom is coming, the earth will rejoice like never before. The gospel will be the best news the world has ever heard.

Preparing the Way

This vision includes key elements for this coming harvest and what the Lord is doing in the church now to prepare for it. This outpouring will ultimately result in some very radical changes for both the church and the world. These need to be understood by those who will be used by God for one of the greatest events in history.

To those who are diligent seekers of God and obedient to His will, what is coming will not be a disruption, but rather a continuation. These things will happen to them as a natural flow of the Spirit and will move them to increased light and intimacy with Him. Those who are comfortable and resist change will have a very hard time. Even so, submission to the Lord, not the circumstances, brings peace and joy, and the peace, joy, and confidence of those who serve the Lord will steadily increase.

We are told in Proverbs 4:18, **"But the path of the righteous is like the light of dawn, that shines brighter and brighter until the full day."** As we walk the path of the righteous, or the right path, our light will grow. It not only makes our own path clearer, so that we can walk with even more boldness and confidence, but it helps illuminate the way for others as well.

Because the Christian life of discipleship is one of ever increasing light, if our life is not this, then somewhere we have missed a turn and left the right path. As C.S. Lewis wrote, "The wrong road never turns into the right road. If we are on the wrong road, then the only way that we can get back on the right road is go back to where we missed the turn." There is nothing greater that we can do to help our loved ones find the Way than staying on it ourselves.

Chapter Two
THE FISHNET

For the coming harvest, the Lord is preparing a great spiritual "fishnet," one able to hold the great catch that is coming. This net is formed by linking together His people in true relationships. The stronger the communication and relationships, the stronger this net will be. It will not only happen in local churches among members, but between local churches, ministries, and movements throughout cities, states, and around the world.

In Ephesians 4:15-16, we see this principle: **"We are to grow up in all aspects into Him, who is the Head, even Christ, from whom the whole body, being fitted and held together by that which every JOINT supplies."** A joint is not a part, but it is where two or more parts come together. A great fitting together is happening in the Spirit now which will increase in the near future on all levels.

Come Together

The Spirit is compelling pastors to get together with other pastors, prophets with prophets, apostles with apostles, and even whole congregations are beginning to visit and interrelate with other congregations apart from their own circles. This is the Lord's doing. Some of these meetings may seem fruitless because of improper agendas, but they will bear fruit and links will be made. Soon the Lord's presence in these meetings will melt all presumption and the façades which separate us from union with Him and each other. His presence will stimulate worship which will bring about a Psalm 133 unity. As we anoint the Head with our worship, the oil will flow down to the edge of His robes, covering the entire body.

He is beginning this breakdown of barriers with the leadership because this is where most barriers originate and where they are the strongest. As these walls come down in the leadership, the entire body will begin to flow together. If the leaders resist this move, the Lord will continue through the congregations. These will begin to relate to other members of the body of Christ, and their bonds will grow stronger regardless of the resistance or warnings of some pastors. The pastors and leaders who continue to resist this tide of unity will be removed from their places. Some will become so hardened they will become opposers and resist God to the end, but most will be changed and repent of their resistance to this irresistible tide of unity.

Because of the magnitude of the "catch," this net will be rent many times and will be in need of constant mending. Much of the discord now taking place in the church is used by the Lord to prepare those whose task in the harvest will be almost exclusively devoted to the mending and binding of this great net. These peacemakers will have a great part in building this net and will have a major impact on the effectiveness of the entire revival. Those who seem to always find themselves in the middle of conflicts should be encouraged with the knowledge that they are being prepared for a great work.

Some who were used greatly by God in the past have become too rigid in doctrinal emphasis or too entangled with spiritual "Ishmaels" to participate in this revival. Some of these will try to join the work, but their interrelationships will be so superficial that they will quickly be torn from the net with the first catch. Those who are linked together by doctrine or who gather around personalities will quickly be torn away. Only those who are joined by and through Jesus will stand the pressure this harvest will bring upon the church (see Colossians 1:17).

The redemption of so many will bring much joy, but it will also come with problems that bring enormous stress to congregations and ministers. The cords of unity must be very strong to withstand this pressure, and they can only be strong to the degree that we abide in the Lord and love one another. Those who have not learned to take the Lord's yoke and try to carry the burdens themselves will be overwhelmed. Entering the Sabbath rest of the Lord will become a major emphasis in preparation for the harvest. Heed this word!

A Revolution

A large number who are now considered Christians, even "Spirit-filled" Christians, have never been led to the Lord. They were led to the church, to a personality, or to a doctrine, but not to the Lord Himself. Some of these will think they are important links in the net but will actually become part of the harvest, starting over again on the proper Foundation—Jesus. This group includes many well-known ministers and pastors. Their humility in this will lead multitudes to question and strengthen their own relationships with the Lord. This will strengthen and encourage the entire body of Christ.

Many denominations, local fellowships, and circles of emphasis will begin disbanding and severing what was built on improper ties, in order to take their place in this great net that the Lord is now forming. For some, these ties will just be ignored or forgotten until they have passed away because of the greater intensity and substance of this new move. For others, it will be a very painful rending as they are persecuted and rejected by those who do not understand. Those who are required to leave much behind will soon receive many times more than what they have left.

Some leaders will actually disband their organizations as they realize that they are no longer relevant to what God is doing. Others will just leave them behind to disband of themselves. Ultimately, all circles of ministry or influence with individual identities will dissolve into a single identity of simply being Christians for all who become part of this harvest. Single presbyteries will form over cities and localities. These will be made up of pastors and leaders from all different backgrounds. Their unity and harmony in purpose, as well as that of the various congregations, will become a marvel to the world.

The Lord will give these presbyteries great wisdom and discernment, but there will be no doubt that Jesus alone will be the Head of His church. What is coming will be bigger than any man or council of men could control or administrate.

The Lord's purpose in preparing for the harvest is to JOIN, not to separate. The dismantling of organizations and disbanding of some works will be a positive and exhilarating experience for the Lord's faithful servants. They will not be just leaving something behind; they will be going on to a much greater work. Those who have fallen to worship the work of God more than the God of the work will have trouble, but most of these will also be set free by the tremendous anointing that is coming.

Stumbling Blocks

Those who feel called to attack and tear down the old will not be sent from the Lord. Many "stumbling blocks" will be circulating in the church who will cause confusion and some destruction from time to time. They will perceive themselves as prophets sent to judge and deliver. Those serving in leadership must trust their discernment and remove the stumbling blocks. These are the "faultfinders" Jude wrote about.

To be distinguished from the "stumbling blocks," the Lord will raise up a great company of prophets, teachers, pastors, and apostles who will be of the spirit of Phinehas. Just as the son of Eleazar could not tolerate iniquity in the camp of the Lord, this "ministry of Phinehas" will save congregations, and at times, even whole nations from the plagues that will be sweeping the earth. They will be moved by the jealousy of the Lord for the purity of His people. They will be sent to save and preserve the work of the Lord, not to tear down as the stumbling blocks so fashion themselves.

Chapter Three
TRIBULATION AND GLORY

For a time, there will be such an inflow of people that even this great net cannot hold them all. Many of the former works and organized churches will be swollen with this overflow. Because of this, they will assert that they are both the cause and primary purpose for this revival. This delusion will not last long because concurrent with the harvest will be gripping tribulation in the world which will eventually consume these works that are not built on the right foundation. This is the judgment of the Lord against the works He did not commission: The great "sea" or mass of humanity, which they sought to rule, will rise up to destroy them.

Lawlessness Increases

Wars will increase. There will even be some nuclear exchanges, but on a limited basis, mostly between third world nations. Far more will perish by plagues and natural disasters than by wars during the period of this vision. The very foundations of civilization will shake and erode. Even the world's most stable governments will be melting like wax, losing authority and control over their populations. Eventually it will be hard to find anyone with the courage to assume authority. This will cause sweeping paranoia throughout the entire earth.

Huge mobs will attack everything in their paths. The infrastructure of the great denominational churches and large visible ministries will be one of their primary targets and will vanish almost overnight. Pagan religions, cults, and witchcraft will spread like plagues, but these will also become targets of the mobs. By this time, governments will have broken down to the point where lynchings and mass executions perpetrated by these mobs are ignored by the authorities. Fear and deep darkness will cover the earth, but this will just make the glory which is appearing upon the saints more striking.

A New Breed of Ministry

In all nations, masses of people will be streaming to the Lord. The inflow will be so great in places that very young Christians will be pastoring large bodies of believers. Arenas and stadiums will overflow nightly as the believers come together to hear the apostles and teachers.

At this time, few congregations will remain separate entities. Many elders and pastors may be stationary, but groups they oversee will be constantly changing. Some of these will be moving on because of persecution and others because the Lord will scatter them to carry His message abroad like seed. Near the end (of the vision), the body of Christ is like a great flowing river sweeping about as freely as the wind. One day there may be meetings in a public auditorium or stadium, the next day in a park, and continually from house to house.

Great meetings that stir entire cities will happen spontaneously. Extraordinary miracles will be common while those considered great today will be performed almost without notice by young believers. Angelic appearances will be common to the saints and a visible glory of the Lord will appear upon some for extended periods of time as power flows through them.

Their unity will be in Jesus, and He alone will be the Head of His church. Eventually, the Lord's presence will be so great during this revival that, like the twenty-four elders in Revelation, all crowns will be cast at His feet and spiritual presumption will be unthinkable.

Those in leadership will be the most humble of all. Those who presume leadership without calling will be apparent to all. The leaders of this move will be true servants, not interested in reputation or position. Their humility will open them to become channels for wave after wave of living water. "He will dwell with the humble of the land."

This harvest will be so great that no one will look back at the early church as a standard, but all will be saying that the Lord has saved His best wine for last. The early church was a firstfruits offering; truly this is the harvest! It was said of the Apostle Paul that he was turning the world upside down; it will be said of the apostles soon to be anointed that they have turned an upside down world right side up. Nations will tremble at the mention of their names.

These men and women of God will take little notice of their own accomplishments because of their burning love for the One working through them and the recognition of His accomplishments. Like Jesus, they will flee to the mountains when men try to make them kings or exalt them improperly. Their exaltation or authority will not come through man; it will only come from above. As the masses will be seeking anyone to take authority during these times, this comes as a warning! If the people make you king, who rules? The authority that the Lord will establish will be very different from what even His own people now perceive. Do not try to rule, just serve. Through this, His authority will flow and begin to bring order though peace.

Chapter Four
EXHORTATIONS FROM THE THRONE

The magnitude of these events cannot be expressed here, neither the chaos nor the move of the Holy Spirit. As to the "rapture," or second appearance of the Lord Jesus, I was not given anything concerning that in this vision. What I was allowed to foresee ended with increasing chaos and increasing revival.

There will be words and exhortations originating from the very throne of the Lord and carrying great authority, coming to prepare His church for the days to come. Not to presume this will be all that He will be saying, but we will soon hear His prophets and teachers begin to emphasize the following:

1. **BUILD UPON THE ONLY FOUNDATION THAT CAN BE LAID, JESUS HIMSELF.** Works that are built upon truths instead of the Truth will not stand. Many congregations and ministries are devastated today by the slightest shaking. The works that are properly built on Jesus will

withstand the greatest trials and attacks without being moved.

There will be a great emphasis on the Lord Jesus Himself in the days to come. The increasing revelation of Him will overshadow the many emphases of the past like the sun overshadows the moon when it rises. The truths that have been such a distraction will begin to seem insignificant as the church begins to see Him **"in whom are hidden ALL of the treasures of wisdom and knowledge" (see Colossians 2:3).**

2. **REMOVE THE BARRIERS AND FACADES THAT SEPARATE US FROM THE LORD AND EACH OTHER.** We must become more intimate with Him and through Him with each other. Spiritual pride and the exaltation of men, individual truths, or works, will come under unrelenting discipline from the Lord and will soon be understood as "strange fire." Those who continue to offer it will perish from the ministry with such demonstration that a pure and holy fear of the Lord will sweep the body of Christ. This will help the church to move into true spiritual worship and a unity which is based on that worship.

3. **ABIDE IN THE SABBATH REST OF THE LORD.** This will become an increasing emphasis in the teaching and a reality as the Lord enters

His temple, the church. Our growing intimacy with Him will bring a peace that will actually calm the storm of the rising sea of humanity. The intensity of the times will overwhelm any pseudo peace. We must be one with the "Lord of the Sabbath."

4. **HEED THE SPIRITUAL PREPARATION WHICH MAY BE REFLECTED IN THE NATURAL.** For example, some have begun moving their assets into precious metals or land. This may be helpful, but it is far more important to take the spiritual land and lay up our treasures in heaven.

The Lord is seeking givers who will become channels of His supply. For them, there will be no lack. Those that hoard or do not learn to freely give may suffer increasing crisis in their earthly affairs. This is the Lord's discipline to set them free. Some who are faithful and generous givers may also experience increasing crisis in this, but it is for their preparation to be great channels for the provision of many. Remember Joseph.

Some are feeling they should limit their travel to certain areas and are beginning to emphasize cleanliness and morality because of the epidemics. This may be helpful, but there is only one deliverance from the judgments of

God—to be found in Christ. Spiritual purity is far more important than the natural and can alone protect us from any plague.

5. **"THE JUST SHALL LIVE BY FAITH," NOT FEAR.** Fears will greatly increase in the world. Actions taken by the church because of fear will almost always prove destructive. Some "faith teaching" has muddied the waters to the degree that some do not even want to hear the word "faith." This frequently happens before the Lord begins a great work. A great revelation of true faith is coming. This will be an essential revelation for us to serve in these days. Some will be called to walk where angels fear to tread. KNOW that He who is in us is MUCH greater than he who is in the world.

The vessels He is now preparing will walk in a boldness and confidence that will astonish a world gripped in fear. Our faith will grow as the presence of the Lord increases. True faith is the recognition of the One in whom we believe. When one truly and properly fears the Lord, he will not fear anything else.

In the coming days, many will exist in the miraculous on a continual basis. This will become as natural to them as the gathering of manna was to Israel. Some of the Lord's exploits on behalf of His people will be unprecedented, exceeding the greatest biblical miracles. These will seem almost normal as they take place because the presence of the Lord will cause more wonderment than His works. He will be very close to His people in these days.

6. **THE LORD WILL SOON OPEN OUR UNDERSTANDING OF HIS WORD AND PURPOSES TO A DEPTH BEYOND OUR PRESENT COMPREHENSION.** The "Books" (of prophecy) are yet to be "opened" as they will be. When they are, our understanding of even basic truths, such as salvation, being born again, etc., will be enormously increased. This will give far more substance and depth of purpose to the entire body of Christ. The functions of the gifts and ministries will come with increasing authority and power as their confidence increases with knowledge.

The spiritual dimension will become more real to the church than the natural. When the proper foundation has been adequately laid in the church (our union and devotion to Jesus Himself), the Spirit of revelation will be poured out as never before.

Honor Fathers and Mothers, But Press On

The charismatic renewal was a notable outpouring, but it seems to many that there was little lasting fruit. Multitudes who met the Lord were lost again to the world, but the Lord did accomplish what He intended. During this movement, there were more churches planted, movements begun, missionaries sent out, and salvations than in any previous move of God in history. Many of those brought into the kingdom remained and matured. He now has what will prove to be a strong foundation to build upon, a net to hold the catch that He has prepared for the end of the age. Through the tribulations and dry times of the last few years, He has carefully been weaving strong cords that He is now beginning to bind together.

Do not resist the Lord in this work. Seek greater intimacy with Him and open yourself to your fellow members in the body of Christ. Reach out to them and remove the barriers. Those who have drifted into extremes will be brought back to the course never again to be distracted from the River of Life by the little tributaries that feed it. Those who have resisted new truth will soon be diving into the River, fearless of rocks or depths. The anointing will soon break all of our yokes. The Reformation showed us the Way. The Pentecostal, Charismatic, and Third Wave renewals began leading us on to Truth. Through the revival that is coming, we will come to know Jesus as our Life. When the cord has all three strands, it will not be easily broken.

This word is given for the PREPARATION of those the Lord desires to use. Relationships are about to be built between ministries and congregations that have feared and rejected each other in the past. He will do this in many without changing their doctrines or emphasis; He will merely cause His people to rise above such differences and worship Him in unity. As He is lifted up, we will gradually begin to wonder how many things that were so important to us and often divided us, could have had so much of our attention. As this final battle begins, we will all be amazed, and sometimes ashamed, at those we find on our side.

Humble yourself under His mighty hand so that you may take part in a great exaltation. Those who allow themselves to be emptied, who lay aside all personal ambition to become of no reputation and patiently suffer rejection and misunderstanding, will soon stir the entire world with the King's message.

THE TITANIC
AND THE
STOCK MARKET

Chapter One
FOUNDATIONS
ARE IMPORTANT

Because this was written at the time of the 1987 stock market crash, which came about the time that the Titanic was found on the bottom of the North Atlantic, the original version of this message focused on those two events. Both of these have prophetic significance and feeling that the message is timeless, and this version was modified slightly to make it more sensitive to present events.

In a sense, the whole world is like the Titanic on that fateful night, still sailing through the darkness in a sea of icebergs. We continue to bump some, scrape by others, repair the damage, and keep going. For this we can be thankful, but we are now in as much, or more, danger than ever. We are still a long way from a safe port. These lessons are as crucial now for us to understand as they have ever been.

To interpret current events in the light of divine purpose has always been a primary function of the prophets. They see the relationship between events in conjunction with God's works and His message. God's prophets do not just foretell or predict, but much of their ministry is devoted to the explanation of signs or messages. Extraordinary events are taking place today that have a message for those who will hear. One of these recent, significant events was the discovery of the Titanic on the bottom of the North Atlantic. This was a divine reminder of conditions and attitudes that can sink the most seemingly unsinkable project, business, ministry, or state.

A Prophetic Parallel

When built, the Titanic was a symbol of the opulence and invincibility that the British Empire felt in those days. She reflected that period's extravagance and arrogance as well as the belief that nothing could sink their expanding world economy and dominion. This attitude is in contrast to God's wisdom that warns: **"Pride goes before destruction, and a haughty spirit before stumbling" (Proverbs16:18).** Few considered His wisdom, and the subsequent catastrophes of both the ship and the empire are now history.

As the Titanic departed on her maiden voyage, Britain could not even conceive that such a fate awaited her and she would never see port again. Neither could many perceive that after one hundred years of freedom from war in Europe that in just two years the entire continent and much of the world would be in the throes of the worst war in history. Their invincible empire was about to hit an iceberg that would ultimately send them to the same end where every one of man's previous empires had gone.

Many in the British clergy encouraged the arrogance of the empire. They preached a conservative patriotism because they saw the empire as the only true protector of the faith and promulgator of the gospel. Their missionaries circled the globe to convert natives in the colonies. Their spiritual heritage was rich. British subjects who refused to compromise their convictions impacted the world with revival and reformation. They also gave the world one of its greatest spiritual gifts—the King James Version of the Bible. They could foresee no other country in the world carrying the mantle of spiritual authority as they had. By the turn of the century, they had reached their limit and were resting more on what they had accomplished than on what was left to do. Pride had replaced vision. When this happens, the end is always near.

The Titanic was just one of many messages the Lord gave Britain to call her to repentance—a repentance that would enable her to continue leading the world toward the fulfillment of His purposes and would give them the opportunity to reach even greater spiritual heights. She did not listen. Now she is firmly entrenched in tradition, her greatness in the past, and the mantle given to another.

Just as the Lord used the British Empire for a period, He has used the United States in a great way. We have possibly even surpassed the British in preaching the gospel. We were used to aid in the reestablishment of Israel as a nation and as the primary hedge against the communist plague. By giving purpose and meaning to the value of the individual and establishing a government devoted to promoting initiative, America rose to become the greatest nation in history. When the U.S. had the power to dominate the world and dictate policy as the lone possessor of nuclear weapons, her esteem for liberty and free determination would not even consider it. She was a nation of pioneers more interested in going somewhere new or making something new than controlling others. The apostle exhorted us to give honor to whom honor is due, and much honor is due to so many who risked their lives, their fortunes, and their sacred honor to give birth to such a nation devoted to liberty.

Now, as painful as it is to see, the handwriting is on our wall. The most destructive thing that could happen to a great nation has happened to the U.S.—vision has been turned into pride. The forward momentum has slowed, and many began to rest more on what has been done than pressing on toward what is left to do. Paul warned the Gentiles, who have been grafted into the vine because of the Jews' hardness of heart, that they could be quickly removed by their own pride. In the same way, pride can remove us from our position in God's purposes. He is able to raise up even the most insignificant nation to take our place. He does not need us; we need Him.

Signs of another great awakening are beginning in the United States. An alarm usually has to be annoying to do its job, and alarms have been sounding that are bringing a righteous agitation. There is yet hope, but let us consider the warnings.

Warning to the United States

The sinking of the Titanic was a warning to Britain to repent of her arrogance, a warning that nothing man could build is invincible. Her discovery on the bottom of the North Atlantic is a timely reminder of just how foolish some of our present arrogance will prove to be if we do not repent of it. The space shuttle catastrophe was another warning to the U.S. The glory of this nation of technological wonders was rising to the heavens one minute, the next she was gone, exactly as the biblical admonition states:

"And I will grant wonders in the sky above, and signs on the earth beneath, blood, and fire, and vapor of smoke" (Acts 2:19).

The nation was shocked and horrified by the blood, the fire, and the vapor of the smoke that the Challenger burned in our hearts that day, but did we get the message? The Lord did not blow up the Challenger, our pride did. Pride breeds carelessness. Without repentance, this nation can evaporate into a few tiny little fragments just as quickly as the Challenger. Economically, we are primed for just such a disaster.

Is there hope for the U.S.? Yes, if there is repentance. With every prophet and warning that the Lord sends to the nations, He sends an appeal for repentance. The judgments foretold are only if they refuse to heed the warning and turn from their wicked ways. This patience on the Lord's part is wonderfully illustrated in the Book of Jonah. The prophet declared that the city was doomed, but the inhabitants repented of their wickedness, entreated the Lord for mercy, and He spared them.

Many prophecies were given in the 1970s about the impending judgment to have come at the turn of the decade. There was a measure of repentance and the Lord gave us more time. Even so, we must not think that because the judgments did not come to pass that the prophecies were not from the Lord. They accomplished the repentance and the Lord gave more time.

This was repeated again in the 1980s, then the 1990s, and again in the 2000s. There were great gatherings in Washington with hundreds of thousands praying, repenting, and asking for divine intervention. If something like this had happened in the Old Testament times, it would be memorialized in canon Scripture. Think about how it would read: "Hundreds of thousands gathered before the king's palace to repent of their sins and call upon the Lord…." This would have been one of the most extraordinary events in the Old Testament, and these certainly gained the attention of heaven—and gave us more time.

It does not take much repentance for the Lord to relent of His intended judgment. When Abraham asked if He would spare Sodom for just ten righteous men, He said that He would. Abraham had begun by asking if there were fifty righteous and kept lowering the number. The Lord did not stop until Abraham did. He is certainly gracious and desires mercy over judgment. For this we should be very thankful, but not become presumptuous.

The repentance experienced by the U.S. seemed hardly measurable to many prophets, but it was enough for the Lord to give us longer. He is inclined to give grace. If there is a measure of turning from the evil that would bring His judgment, and the Lord relents again for a period of time, will we be like Jonah and mourn because the Lord did not bring down His fire? Are we going to be discouraged and refuse to keep prophesying?

No. Let us speak His words with boldness while praying for the people to hear and repent. A single soul is worth more than the ridicule we might suffer because of the perception that our prophecies did not come to pass. How much more an entire nation? We should pray for repentance that these things will not have to come to pass now. About the present warnings many are saying today, "We've heard that all before and nothing happened." They do not understand why nothing happened. The Scriptures are clear that times of trouble will come upon the world, so we should always be ready but also thankful for the peace when we have it.

It is right to pray for repentance and peace, but prepare for troubles. If the troubles come, we know the kingdom is that much closer, so we have cause for rejoicing either way. We must not be like the foolish virgins who decided to sleep because the Lord seemed to delay His coming. If He gives us another year or fifty, let us use the time wisely. Even if we have fifty more years, we do not have time to waste.

Even with the large prayer and repentance movements, the troubles and the dangers in the world have increased. In the United States, the wickedness that brings judgment has also increased. The repentance must go beyond the sorrow and willingness to gather in events but must translate into a change of behavior. At present, the ultimate depravity of "calling good evil, and evil good, honoring the dishonorable while dishonoring the honorable," is gaining an increasing grip on the United States, which still claims to be over 80 percent Christian. Large gatherings are no longer enough—we must have revival in America.

The Pride of Man

It is hard not to marvel constantly at the inventions of mankind. It is right that we should be impressed with them and to give honor to those whom honor is due for helping to make the modern world much more comfortable and easy. Invention and creativity were put in man as the image of his Creator who rejoices in creativity. However, when we start to think that it is our own wisdom and power apart from our Creator, the same pride enters into man that entered into Satan and caused the first fall and most of them since.

The world's wealthy and famous streamed onto the Titanic for her maiden voyage. Man actually thought he had built something that could not sink. It was almost as foolish as the men of Shinar who thought they could build a tower that would reach heaven. Because they didn't think their ship could sink, they sailed boldly into dangerous waters with reckless abandon. This "unsinkable" pride of the empire proved to be very fragile, just like the empire itself, just like every empire. In relation to the present world economy, it has been repeated often and believed by many that the kind of crash which happened in 1929 could never happen again. It is said there are too many safeguards, a stronger Federal Reserve, higher margin requirements for speculators and institutions, FDIC, FSLIC, SIPC, and so on. Do not believe it. We are more vulnerable to a worldwide economic catastrophe than at any time in history, and we are merrily sailing along in the most treacherous seas. The Fed, FDIC, and all of the other safeguards are lifeboats that may save a few, but they are wholly inadequate for the voyage we're on.

The owners of the Titanic felt that carrying even half the lifeboats for a ship her size was superfluous. Today's leaders are sailing with the same disdain of reason while touting their ingenuity in designing a ship they think cannot sink. In October 1987, we hit an iceberg. We hit another with the "dot.com crash" in the 1990s, and another with the terrible blow we took from the September 11 World Trade Center attack. We banged into another economic iceberg in 2008. Each time the ship of state was repaired and continued to sail. We should all be thankful for this, but this by no means guarantees that the next one won't be even more devastating, even to the sinking of the ship. No state, no economy, is unsinkable. The world economy is now very battered and just limping along. It could grind to a stop or start taking on water faster than it can be pumped out at any time.

It is a repeated truth that those who do not know history are doomed to repeat it. Students of history marvel at the repetitious cycles of human mistakes. Few have been able to break out of these cycles. Few have been wise enough to see anything but what they wanted to see in the trends and events taking place around them. This has also been the case with many who were called as prophets to warn the world and the church. As it was with the biblical seers, those calling for repentance will be lonely voices. The majority who claim to be messengers will always be found preaching prosperity and peace; the majority always has been more concerned about their acceptance than the truth of the message.

Those in authority, by the nature of their power, feel compelled to put the worst face on the problems of their predecessors and the best face on the problems they create. Only the most courageous leaders have been able to hear the warnings and take action before the problems reached crisis levels. Empire after empire, nation after nation, churches, organizations, companies, and even families, continue to fail because their leaders refuse to face the problems until they are beyond control.

It is sobering how the reactions of the politicians and experts after the stock market crash of October

1987 and the subsequent economic blows echoed the voices of October 1929. In some cases, you wondered if they were reading from a history book. After the crash in 1929, the first response of the politicians was to point out the "underlying health of the economy." Christmas sales that year were as brisk as ever. The crash was soon almost forgotten, remembered as a curiosity more than anything else. After the crash, the market began to rise again and continued for almost three years, until June 1932, when the Depression actually began.

Even though it was under the surface for awhile, the economy began unraveling in '29; the ship of state was taking on water. Pressure rose for the government to do something. As much as they tried to do what Wall Street demanded, everything they did only exacerbated the problem. As it turned out, the underlying health of the economy was far sicker than anyone had foreseen.

When the Titanic hit the iceberg, there was a disconcerting jolt. Almost everyone felt it, but after a minute or two, the party continued. No one could imagine that in just a few hours most of them would be on the bottom of the North Atlantic. The ship was just so big and luxurious, and all of the experts said it was unsinkable. The Lord Jesus and Paul both warned us that the final catastrophe of the age would be just like this, just as it was in the days of Noah.

"For as in those days which were before the flood they were eating and drinking, they were marrying and giving in marriage, until the day that Noah entercd the ark,

and they did not understand until the flood came and took them all away" (Matthew 24:38-39).

While they are saying, "Peace and safety!" then destruction will come upon them suddenly.

But you, brethren, are not in darkness, that the day should overtake you like a thief (I Thessalonians 5:3-4).

The stock market is usually a thermometer which continually takes the temperature of business. It reflects the values that the world puts on the economy. Occasionally, it has become a thermostat, setting the direction and pace of business. When that happens, it is usually catastrophic. Not since October 1929 has this begun to happen so frequently with the stock market leading the economy instead of reflecting it.

As Roger Smith, the Chairman of General Motors, stated when asked about the 1987 turmoil on Wall Street: "We didn't just have a tummy ache here in our country; we had a genuine, certified heart attack! If you don't recognize it as a heart attack, and if you don't get on that diet and start doing your exercise, you can have another one and it could be terminal."

2008 and Beyond

Twenty-one years passed from the Stock Market Crash of 1987 to the crash of 2008. There were some bumps during that time, and the unprecedented challenge of the 9/11 terrorist attacks and subsequent war on terror, but for the most part these two decades seemed to be a time of stabilizing and almost boundless prosperity for the West. Much of the prosperity had been built on a real estate bubble created by subprime lending. The day of reckoning came in the fall of 2008, and the world has tottered on the edge of economic collapse since. Now instability is the norm with wild swings in virtually every market becoming common.

The economic force is often referred to as an "engine" because it parallels the operation of an engine. It has many parts that must work together and needs fuel to run. As a jet pilot, I learned to pay close attention to my engine instruments and know what they were indicating. Even if the particular systems were staying within their tolerances, certain trends could foretell serious problems. If there are oscillations, even though they stay within parameters, the engine may not just quit, it could explode. The economic instruments of the entire world are not only wildly oscillating, but they have long ago, and by a large margin, departed their safe parameters.

Because world leaders have failed to address some of the most basic economic problems, the prospect of a fast, even instantaneous meltdown of the world economy has gone from a possibility to a probability. There are now several crises that could cause this. With currencies no longer backed by anything but faith in the governments issuing them, just one major player refusing to take them anymore could begin the panic that unravels the entire monetary system. It is that fragile now.

In 1987, I was shown that bartering would be the currency for a period of time. At the time, this seemed farfetched, but now it seems imminent. Believers all over the world have been hearing that they should have food and water supplies that could last several months. This seems very prudent.

Jim Bakker began encouraging Christians to get prepared in this way years ago. He prophesied the Katrina disaster several weeks before the storm hit and not many listened. He prophesied the 2011 Japan earthquake and tsunami several weeks before it struck, and some Japanese listened and ordered food to store. When the disaster struck, they sent pictures with the story of how their neighbors had to stand in line many hours a day for provisions, and they did not have to stand in lines, but rather had that time for ministry. When disaster strikes, it will be harvest time and the prepared will save many.

Eyes to See

The Titanic received numerous warnings about the ice field which lay directly across their path, and they did not even slow down. Even if they were unsinkable, to hit an iceberg head-on would almost certainly cause great damage and loss of life. After the tragedy, it was reported that the lookouts had requested binoculars and were refused them. In the hearings after the disaster, it was determined that if they had been given binoculars it is likely this tragedy would have been averted. Today we have a similar condition in the church, with very few being willing to invest the little that it takes to raise up and equip true watchmen who can see.

When the first rescue ship arrived in the morning, they were astonished at how far into the ice field the Titanic had gone without hitting an iceberg. They had difficulty getting to the Titanic's position in daylight because of the great number of icebergs. The only possible reason for Smith's proceeding with such disdain for the danger is an incredible false sense of security.

When one looks at the course of Western economic policy for the last few decades, one must also wonder what our leaders were thinking, and how we possibly survived without a catastrophe this long. The only answer is that the Lord truly has His angels holding back the four winds of the earth until His bondservants are ready (see Revelation 7:1).

It does appear that we have come to the time when the world will go through the greatest troubles ever known—but these are also birth pangs for the coming of a new age, one in which our King will reign. He exhorted us to know the signs of the times and to be prepared. This is not just to save ourselves, but we are called to take action. There is much for us to do, but we will not be able to save others if we are drowning ourselves.

Because they believed the hype and vain boasts of the engineers and owners, the Titanic's crew never held a proper lifeboat drill. They did not have a plan for the orderly movement of passengers to the boats, and most of the crew did not even know how to lower them. Everything had to be learned while the ship was sinking under their feet. This obviously contributed to a much greater loss of life than was necessary. Many boats were lowered only partially full, one with only twelve people. Many passengers did not believe the ship could sink and refused to leave the comfort and warmth of their cabins. Hundreds of those willing to abandon her were held below decks until it was too late. The entire ship had been caught off guard by the events of that fateful night, and they paid dearly for it. Will we be caught in the same position? The Lord exhorted us to know the signs of the times and not to sleep on our watch. Prophets throughout the land are now calling for PREPARATION; the Lord is giving us signs in the heavens and on the earth. He is NOW loading His lifeboat.

"TODAY if you hear His voice, do not harden you hearts" (see Hebrews 4:7).

Therefore, let everyone who is godly pray to You in a time when You may be found; surely in a flood of great waters they shall not reach him (Psalm 32:6).

In coming years, devastating economic problems will be sweeping the world in waves. Great countries and societies will be collapsing. Like the passengers on the Titanic, the water will lap at our ankles, then our knees, and then there will be a mad rush to the highest part of the ship. It will all be in vain; the whole ship is going to sink. The entire world system is near the end, but we don't have to go down with this ship, because we don't have to be on it.

Be Prepared

So what do we do? SEEK THE LORD! I do not mean seek Him for instructions as to what we should do—seek Him because HE IS what we should do.

He is the Ark of God in whom we will be delivered from every flood. He Himself bore the curse of our sins and absorbed the judgment that was ours. If we are abiding in Him, we do not have to fear the judgment against sin. This does not mean that we will not be here or will not have to endure trials. It does mean that even if we are called to walk through the fire, it will not burn us. The floods may come, but our house will be built upon a Rock that can sustain any storm. For years, doctrines have been preached which have lulled the church into a deep sleep. They did this by assuring us that those in Christ would not have to go through troubles. This is contrary to the entire testimony of Scripture. He said that in the world we would have tribulation, and that **"through many tribulations we must enter the kingdom of God" (see Acts 14:22).**

In every trial there is a doorway to the kingdom. When the world goes through "the great tribulation," it will be the doorway through which the entire world enters the kingdom. We see this in places such as Isaiah 60. As written, while darkness is covering the earth and deep darkness the people, God's glory will be rising on His people. As we see in verse 3, the world will come to the light. The light is going to win!

Let us consider, would it be better to be prepared and not have to go through tribulation or to not be prepared and have to go through it? The Lord exhorted us to be ready and watching—to be prepared. We cannot continue with the delusions of the Titanic crew who did not think that adversity could come to them—because then it will. No Scripture says we will be raptured before tribulation. There obviously is a time when those who are Christ's will be changed and caught up to meet Him as He returns, but nowhere does it say when except at His return. Many have based their entire hope on the conjecture of a few men and women when the whole Bible is a testimony of God's deliverance and victory through tribulation, not from it.

As Corrie ten Boom once declared: "I have been in countries where the saints are already suffering terrible persecution. In China, the Christians were told, 'Don't worry, before the tribulation comes, you will be translated—raptured.' Then came a terrible persecution, and millions of Christians were tortured to death. Later I heard a Bishop from China say, sadly, 'We have failed. We should have made the people strong for persecution rather than telling them Jesus would come first.' Turning to me he said, 'You will have time. Tell the people to be strong in times of persecution, how to stand when tribulation comes—to stand and not faint.'"

There is a kingdom that cannot be shaken, that cannot sink. It is a kingdom so great and so powerful that if all of the greatest problems and tragedies in history were afflicted upon it at once, it may not even be enough to get the attention of a single inhabitant. In the expanse of God's universe, the entire earth compares as less than a single drop would to all the world's oceans. Except for the tiny little speck called earth, the goodness of God dominates the universe. He is in control, and He cares about this little speck. He even cares about you and me. He has called us to live under His dominion now. In His kingdom all things work together for good (see Romans 8:28); in all things we overwhelmingly conquer through Him (see Romans 8:37); He always leads us in His triumph in Christ (see II Corinthians 2:14).

If we have the true fear of the Lord, we need not fear anything else. The Lord clearly told us how we can build our houses on the rock that will endure the storm (see Matthew 7:24-27). There are only two requirements—to hear His words and then to act on them, but we must do both.

Follow Him

As we see in John 10, His sheep know His voice, and they follow Him because they know His voice. I read an account of three shepherds in the Middle East who brought their herds to a watering hole at the same time. As the shepherds talked, the sheep began to mingle. To the amazement of the writer, the shepherds seemed unconcerned that it may be impossible to ever get the herds sorted out again.

When it was time for them to depart, each man took a different path and began to sing as he went. There was a huge convulsion in the mixed herd; then little streams of sheep began to follow after each shepherd until they had all separated. Though all of the shepherds were singing, each sheep knew his own master's voice.

Many voices in the world lead down many different paths. We must know our Master's voice so well that even if all are speaking at the same time, we hear His voice and follow Him only. All of the paths may look good, but we cannot follow a path, we must follow Him. If we walk by formulas, we can be easily misled. It is not enough to know someone who knows His voice, but we must know Him ourselves.

The only way you can know His voice so as to distinguish it from all of the others is to spend time with Him. I could describe my wife's voice to you, but you probably could not distinguish her by just that description if she were in a group who were all speaking. I would instantly know her voice because we have been together for so long. The same is true with the Lord. Studying ways to know His voice cannot substitute for just being with Him.

If we try to comprehend and identify the many voices of the evil one, we will be confused and frustrated. I was told about a law enforcement officer who spent each day handling true U.S. currency. After a time he knew the feel of each bill so well that he would immediately recognize counterfeit bills when he touched them. That's how well we must know the Lord's voice.

High-Impact, Low-Maintenance Christians

Every Christian should be a high-impact, low-maintenance person when they have matured in Christ. We should be able to not only bear our own burdens but also help others. At present, far too many Christians are low impact, high maintenance, able to give very little help to others, while requiring a lot of help themselves.

This is especially true in the area of finances, and more people are becoming dependent on the state to be able to make it. We are specifically warned about this in biblical prophecy concerning the end of this age, and this will ultimately result in the worst form of tyranny for those who have become subject to it.

There is a reason why the "mark of the beast" is a financial mark that determines whether we can buy, sell, or trade in this world. The harvest, which is the end of the age, is the maturing of everything that has been sown in man, both the good and the evil. One of the ultimate evils we are told is "the love of money." This is because money is the primary false god in this world. A false god is not just something we bow down to physically, but with our heart and our hope. A false god is something we put our trust in that eclipses our trust in God.

The biblical disciplines of moderation and being able to provide for our own will be keys to spiritual and economic survival as we get closer to the end of the age. A key to this is the biblical discipline of tithing, giving the first 10 percent of our earnings to the Lord. Many believe that this is not required in the New Testament, and I understand this argument, having heard it many times, but if you are prone to believe this please consider the following. Tithing is so important that at the end of this age, it will be a life and death issue.

First, you do not have to believe in tithing to be saved, but it is a basic discipline of those who have walked with God, before the Law, under the Law, and it is established in the New Covenant as well. Even Abraham paid a tithe to Melchizedek. Every New Covenant believer is called to the Melchizedek priesthood, and Melchizedek received tithes. The enigmatic Melchizedek priesthood cannot be fully understood without understanding this basic factor.

We also see in the very first mention in Scripture that God has a house, when Jacob had the dream of the ladder that reached into heaven (which is the most basic purpose of God's house—to be a place of access to heaven). Jacob's response to this revelation was that of all that God blessed him with, he would give a tenth back to God (see Genesis 28:10-28). It can be established that this will always be a result of those who have a true revelation of the house of God.

Many things are revealed by God about His righteousness and justice that were before the Law, and were included in the Law, and are still required of those who would serve Him. Loving God and loving one another were part of the Law, and they are still basic to those who follow Him and serve Him. The Lord did not like murder, adultery, or stealing, etc. before the Law, and just because these are in the Law and under the New Covenant, and we no longer seek to keep the Law for our righteousness, these are still abhorrent to God and will not be practiced by those who love Him and seek to serve Him.

There is not enough space to give this the attention that it deserves, but having been in ministry on some level for nearly forty years, I don't think I have ever met a high-impact, low-maintenance Christian who did not believe in tithing as a basic responsibility of those who trust the Lord. Therefore, I've sought to understand the connection. I have never met a Christian who was faithful in tithing who had chronic financial problems. They occasionally may hit some economic bumps or go through tight times, but the overall strength of their financial condition is strong. I think this is connected to the reason why the Lord said that He could not trust us with the true riches of the kingdom if we do not handle unrighteous mammon well.

I have talked to a number of Christian financial counselors who have learned that the first question to ask anyone who comes to them with financial problems is if they are faithful to tithe. Every one who comes to them with financial problems is not faithful in this, without exception. I have talked to a number who will not counsel anyone on financial matters who does not believe in tithing because they do not believe they can help them in a lasting way if they do not get this basic principle of tithing right.

Some estimates are that from one-third to one-half of the references to righteousness in Scripture have to do with stewardship. His kingdom is built on the pillars of righteousness and justice. Giving to God first what is due to Him is fundamental to both of these and a life that is built on His kingdom.

The Perfect Law of Liberty

We are not under the yoke of the Law if we trust Christ and His atonement sacrifice for our salvation.

That is clear, and we must never compromise it. However, just because we are no longer under the Law does not mean that we are above the Law.

As discussed above, since "you shall not kill" was a commandment in the Law, does that mean that we can kill now that we are no longer "under the Law"? Did the Lord approve of adultery before the Law, or does He approve of it now? Of course not. These are God's standards of righteousness that existed before the Law and after. That we now trust the Lord for our forgiveness and our salvation does not mean that we are now free to do these things. As the Apostle Paul remarked concerning those who thought that they could now sin so that grace could abound: **"Their condemnation is just" (see Romans 3:8).**

However, to make anything like tithing a requirement for inclusion in the congregation of believers is a form of legalism we must reject. We can disagree about it, but we must not divide over it. We also need to challenge those who hold to different positions and who are on different levels of maturity for all of us to mature in the ultimate purpose we all have—loving God and therefore loving His people as well. We should strongly hold to what we believe is true, without compromise, but also do this with grace and mercy toward those who may not see things the way we do.

Trends are revealed in the Scriptures that we must confront and reject in the church. For example, responsible leaders must "mark those who cause divisions"—those who may hold to positions strongly but also pressure and demand that others see things as they do. As we see in the Book of Jude, we need to reject "faultfinders" who obviously have a terrible destiny. There is a saying that "anyone can kick a barn down, but it takes a skillful carpenter to build one." The Apostle Paul had authority for building up and tearing down, but he only had the authority to tear down because he had been a successful builder. We must beware of the faultfinders.

Another trend that was revealed to be the nature of the serpent in the beginning is to be "crafty." These are the ones who are always looking for a loophole, who are always trying to bend the rules and see how much they can get away with, rather than having the nature of Christ that is in every way seeking to obey.

This may just be my experience, but I do have quite a vast experience that has crossed many denominations and movements in the body of Christ concerning tithing, but it is my experience to date. I have received some thoughtful emails and letters from those who had sincere questions about New Covenant tithing and addressed what I think are legitimate questions about how some seem to be using tithing legalistically and manipulatively. They had sincere questions, not an agenda. Most that I know who have an agenda to brand tithing as legalism or putting Christians under the yoke of the Law have a history of causing divisions, and they also have been prone to chronic financial problems and a burden to other Christians. We must evaluate such things on the basis of judging them by their fruit. What have they built that gives them their authority? What does their own life look like?

Those who are still of this nature will always be able to find an excuse, from "that's Old Covenant," to "every thing I have is the Lord's," so they don't give anything. The Lord does not usually go out of His way to convince such people because you can't. Even so, consider this if you are of that opinion: There are only two brief, obscure references in the whole Bible to such an important matter as being born again. Some of the most important issues are addressed briefly, or obscurely, but to those who want to obey, they will be bright, clear, and loud.

It should not be a burden but a privilege to give back to the Lord. Certainly He does not need it, but we need to be generous, and He knows well that where our treasure is there will our hearts be also. If we are not willing to put our treasure into His house, or His work, then our hearts are not really with Him in them.

Without a doubt, the waters have been muddied by the abuse and extreme use of these teachings that are made by some. However, the Lord allows this kind of thing to test us, and those who are true to Him will see clearly enough regardless of how muddy the waters become at times. Manipulation, hype, and pressuring are not only beneath the dignity of the Lord and His true servants, they are a form of witchcraft, which is counterfeit spiritual authority. If we are going to be true, we will not respond to manipulation and pressuring, but we will seek the right place to give because our hearts want to give to the work of the Lord.

Many teachings on giving seem to feed selfishness, but some of these are from the Lord. How is that? First, many Scriptures encourage us to give out of what appears to be selfish reasons, too. Why? Because children are immature and selfish. Becoming less selfish and having higher, more noble purposes is a part of spiritual maturity, but when we are born again we will not be mature. The Word of God is filled with milk for young believers. Let's consider some of these in relation to giving and generosity:

> **"Give, and it will be given to You" (see Luke 6:38).**

> **Honor the Lord from your wealth, and from the first of all your produce;**

so your barns will be filled with plenty, and your vats will overflow with new wine (Proverbs 3:9-10).

There is one who scatters, yet increases all the more, and there is one who withholds what is justly due, but it results only in want.

The generous man will be prosperous, and he who waters will himself be watered (Proverbs 11:24-25).

"Will a man rob God? Yet you are robbing Me! But you say, 'How have we robbed Thee?' In tithes and offerings.

"You are cursed with a curse, for you are robbing Me, the whole nation of you!

"Bring the whole tithe into the storehouse, so that there may be food in My house, and test me now in this," says the Lord of hosts, "if I will not open for you the windows of heaven, and pour out for you a blessing until it overflows" (Malachi 3:8-10).

The Lord Himself said, **"The Scripture cannot be broken" (see John 10:35),** and everywhere in the New Testament that "the Scriptures" are referred to, it is in reference to what we call "the Old Testament." If you need a reference from the New Testament, there's a good one in II Corinthians 9:6-10:

Now this I say, he who sows sparingly shall also reap sparingly; and he who sows bountifully shall also reap bountifully.

Let each one do just as he has purposed in his heart; not grudgingly or under compulsion; for God loves a cheerful giver.

And God is able to make all grace abound to you, that always having all sufficiency in everything, you may have an abundance for every good deed;

as it is written, "He scattered abroad, he gave to the poor, His righteousness abides forever."

Now He who supplies seed to the sower and bread for food, will supply and multiply your seed for sowing and increase the harvest of your righteousness.

All of these Scriptures appeal to benefits we receive for our obedience. These blessings should be received with thanksgiving. It is true that as we mature we should have higher motives, but only the deluded or self-righteous will reject these because they think they are above this. However, the highest purpose for having what we give multiplied back to us should be to have even more seed for sowing. Our goal should not be to just increase our standard of living, but rather increase our standard of giving.

I do not apologize for making some decisions with mine and my family's financial health in mind. The main thing I do for this is tithe. There is no better, more safe, more profitable investment we can ever make. I personally feel that one has to be supremely deceived in some way not to take advantage of what God Himself promises.

I do not want to belabor this point too much, even though I do consider it essential for basic spiritual health because "the love of money is the root of all evil" (literal translation of I Timothy 6:10). Again, this is why the "mark of the beast" is an economic mark. Money can be the ultimate idol of the human heart—what we put our trust in instead of God.

As an instrument flight instructor, I had to teach what was called the "instrument scan." This is the skill of developing a pattern for scanning all of the instruments so you don't become preoccupied with one and lose control of the others. When a pilot's scan starts to deteriorate, the altitude control always seems to be the first to go. When this is corrected, everything else will usually fall into place again. I have found the same thing to be true spiritually— when there is overall disorientation, it usually begins with our attitude or carelessness in giving. With few exceptions, when this is corrected, everything else starts falling into place.

How we handle the resources we have been entrusted with will obviously be a key factor at the end of this age. As we see in the Parable of the Talents, this is what will have us either called "wicked, evil slave" or "good and faithful servant" at the judgment.

The Kingdom Is Coming!

The world systems and governments are already sinking. In Scripture, mountains are often symbolic of governments and the sea speaks of the mass of humanity (see Revelation 17:15; Isaiah 17:12-13). As it says in Psalm 46:2, the mountains will slip into the sea—but we shall not fear. In the days to come, all governments will be melting like wax (see Psalm 97:5), and for a time, the shifting seas that are in great confusion and turmoil will begin washing them away. However, God's government will not be moved—it will be growing stronger and larger in the earth as all others dissolve. We must keep in mind that His kingdom is not *of* this world, but is very different than the governments of this world.

The doctrine of the kingdom is yet to be preached. The doctrine of salvation has gone into most of the world but not the gospel of the kingdom. Some today are preaching *a* doctrine of the kingdom, but we have not yet heard *the* message of the kingdom. When this unfolds and becomes the clear trumpet call, then we will know that the end of this age is near and the beginning of the restoration of the earth will be soon.

In Scripture, the first son born was often rejected as the heir, and the second was chosen. We see this from Cain and Abel through the patriarchs and then throughout the history of the Old Testament. When the kingdom was established in Israel as a type of the kingdom of God, there had to be a Saul before David. This is a message that the first to appear may not be the one. For this reason, we should not automatically believe the first message of the kingdom that comes along and appears to be head and shoulders above the rest. Even David, whose throne is to endure for the ages that the Lord Himself is seated upon, did not have the appearance of a king, even to the great prophet Samuel. The kingdom will come far more subtly than we are being led to believe. As Jesus warned the Pharisees, who had very carefully laid out their doctrines on the coming kingdom of the Messiah, **"The kingdom of God does not come with observation" (see Luke 17:20 NKJV).**

Though we may not yet know exactly how it is coming to the earth, we know that it is, and we know how to prepare for it. We know that we can begin to live in the kingdom now—by abiding in the King and obeying His will. If we are abiding in Him, we will be prepared. We have come to the most exciting and significant time in history that even the prophets and righteous of old desired to see. We have been given the privilege of living in them, and we are here for a purpose.

Three Ships and Three Types of Leadership

In prophetic dreams and visions, ships often represent leader-*ship*. Two other ships played a significant role in the drama of the Titanic disaster: the Californian and the Carpathia. Together, these three ships and their captains remarkably parallel the prevailing attitudes in leadership today.

The Californian obviously had a reserved and cautious captain. When he heard about the ice in his path, he slowed down. When he saw the ice, he ordered the ship to be stopped and waited for daylight. His wireless (radio) operator began warning the other ships in the area of the danger. At 7:30 p.m., her warning was received and logged by the Titanic. This professional, reserved, and cautious captain possibly saved his own ship by following his nature that night, but later his caution possibly cost the lives of those who perished on the Titanic.

The Titanic crew received six warnings about the ice that night and disregarded them all. This reveals the arrogant casualness that permeated her bridge. It was not just the captain, but almost the entire officer staff who received and paid little or no attention to the warnings. When this attitude prevails in the leadership, the disregard of authoritative warnings, doom is imminent.

The usually stormy North Atlantic was amazingly calm that night. One officer remarked that he had never seen the sea so tranquil. First officer Lightoller of the Titanic made this observation at the inquiry when he declared that "everything was against us." The Lord warned, **"When men shall say 'peace and safety' sudden destruction will come" (see I Thessalonians 5:3).** The world economy is right now sailing through the most dangerous waters. The further we go and the deeper into the minefield of icebergs we get, the harder it will be to get out of it.

This tranquility must have also overcome the crew of the Californian. Her bridge watch saw the Titanic approaching just a few miles away. Then saw her stop dead in the water. At first, they thought she was taking the same precautions for the ice which they had taken. Then she started firing rockets into the air every few minutes, always a distress signal at sea. They rationalized this saying that it must be a signal meant for another company ship that they could not see. The wireless operator was asleep, and they did not even wake him to see if he could contact the Titanic and confirm this theory. Then they watched her disappear, telling each other that she was sailing away when she was actually slipping beneath the sea.

Had the crew of the Californian responded to the first distress signal, they may well have been able to save all of the lives that were lost. The lackadaisical attitude of her crew that night is beyond comprehension, just as is the attitude of world leaders and even many church leaders today. When the final inquiry comes and the final story is told, are we going to marvel and lament at how many we could have saved but did not? The crew of the Californian was subject to the indignation of the world for sleeping through the greatest tragedy ever at sea when they could have done so much. Are we going to sleep right through the greatest of all tragedies when we could have done much?

Rationalization is a popular shield for cowards. Were they so afraid of the ice that they decided to humor each other with such unbelievable reasons for not responding to an obvious emergency? Let us consider the most sobering exhortation of Revelation 21:8: **"But for the cowardly and unbelieving and abominable and murderers and immoral persons and sorcerers and idolaters and all liars, their part *will be* in the lake that burns with fire and brimstone, which is the second death."** Here we see that the **"cowardly"** are the first to be thrown into the lake of fire. There is no place for cowardice in Christianity.

The other ship in the fateful drama of that night was the Carpathia, captained by Arthur H. Rostron.

He was known for his ability to make quick decisions while energizing those who served under him. He was a pious man devoted to prayer. At 12:35 a.m., the Carpathia's wireless operator burst into Rostron's quarters to report that the Titanic had struck an iceberg. Rostron reacted in character. He ordered the Carpathia turned toward the disaster and full speed ahead, later asking the operator if he was sure of the message, a striking contrast to the reaction on the Californian.

Rostron then gave an amazing display of a truly prepared mind. He seemed to think of everything. He ordered the English doctor to the first-class dining room, the Italian doctor to second-class, the Hungarian to third-class, along with every possible piece of equipment or supplies needed for the sick or wounded. He ordered different officers to different gangways, instructing them to get the names of survivors to send by wireless. They prepared block and lines with chair slings for the wounded. Bowlines were secured along the ship's sides, along with boat ropes and heaving lines, for securing people in chairs. All gangway doors were opened. He then directed specific officers to be in charge of his present passengers, to take care of their needs and keep them out of the way. All hands were to prepare coffee, soup, and provisions. He then designated that all officer's cabin's, smoke rooms, library, etc., be used to accommodate the survivors.

Stewards were sent to reassure and explain to their own passengers the reason for the activity to help keep them calm.

Then Rostron turned to face the biggest problem of all—the ice. He was heading at full speed into the same field that had sunk the Titanic. To him reducing speed was out of the question, but he took every measure to reduce the risk to his own ship and passengers. He added a man to the crow's nest, put two more on the bow, one on each wing of the bridge, and he stayed there himself. His second officer, James Bisset, then watched the captain taking one last most important measure—he prayed.

At 2:45 a.m., Bisset saw the first iceberg. They steered around it and kept going. The next hour they dodged five more. At 4:00 a.m., they reached the Titanic's last called position and began picking up lifeboats. As the sun rose it revealed an astonishing sight; the sea was full of icebergs for as far as the eye could see. Even with all the lookouts, the Carpathia had passed numerous ones they had not even seen. No one could imagine how they missed them all, except the captain, who knew well who the Holy Spirit was—the Helper, not the Doer.

The difficult rescue of the survivors was carried out with such order and discipline that peace reigned over all. The Carpathia's passengers caught the spirit of self-sacrifice. The first-class passengers gave their own quarters to survivors; others were pitching in to do all they could. On one of the darkest nights of tragedy ever experienced on the high seas, the Carpathia's captain, crew, and passengers stand out as bright lights of courage and heroism. They are a demonstration of what the Lord has called us to be in the night of tragedy and loss that is now falling upon the earth. Let us not sleep as some did or be fooled by the present calmness of the sea; let us be PREPARED. As the prophet Daniel foresaw, **"The people who know their God will display strength and take action" (see Daniel 11:32).**

The three types of leadership are: 1) the proud and reckless, 2) the dull and cowardly, 3) the wise and the prepared. Which will we be?

NOTE FOR THE 2008 EDITION:

(I have kept this 2008 note in the 2012 edition because it was significant that it was published just months before the 2008 crash. This warning applies now as much as it did then.)

True kingdom principles can be applied on any level or any time. The principles addressed in this vision can be applied to individuals, businesses, governments, or even the world.

In Revelation 11:15, we are told that the kingdom of this world becomes the kingdom of our Lord. This implies a transformation. For this reason, we should always hope that a nation could make the transformation instead of being totally washed away in the flood that is even now lashing the earth. We can expect whatever part of those nations, which is built on hearing and obeying the Word of the Lord, to remain. However, there is a "holy nation," the church, which we should be even more concerned about, even out of love for our nations. If the "salt loses its savor," or the light that the church is called to have ceases to shine, the nations do not have a chance.

In using the prophetic metaphor of the Titanic and the icebergs, the 1987 stock market crash is now more than two decades in the past. Has the U.S. avoided the tragedy this warning was originally given for? I think in some ways we have been able to navigate through some very treacherous waters, but we are not out of them yet. We have also bumped and scraped some icebergs with some damage, such as with the dot.com crash in the 1990s and the economic slam caused by the attack on the World Trade Center in 2001. After both of these, the ship has righted itself, the repairs have been made, and we continue on, seemingly stronger and wiser than ever. For this, we should be very thankful. We have been given much grace.

However, we need to acknowledge this as grace. Even the experts still do not seem to understand how we have come through all that we have, which one can easily see by watching the business news programs for the continual conflicts and contradictions of opinions. We must not be lulled to sleep; the watchmen and the crew must remain alert.

Now we have the constant pressure of terrorism, the almost constant conflict in the Middle East, potentially a major showdown looming with some rogue states such as Iran, and tragedies such as the devastating hurricanes. Through all of this, the wisdom of our leaders and the strength and resilience of the U.S. and world economies have been nothing short of remarkable. Again, for all of this we should be very thankful. However, again we are far from being out of the ice field. In fact, the icebergs seem to be even more numerous now than ever with rogue states gaining nuclear weapons and radical Islam continuing to grow in both numbers and resolve to bring down Western civilization.

We may think that the U.S. is essential to God's plans, but it is not. He can raise up the smallest and weakest of nations to do all that we are doing. Pride is the bomb we should fear the most. However, even if all the economies of all the nations collapsed, there is a kingdom that cannot be shaken, which cannot sink—the kingdom of God—and those who have built their lives on that kingdom have nothing to fear from anything that happens in this world.

As it was stated in this vision that it would happen, fear is growing in the world. Many problems are growing beyond human remedy. This will make it increasingly apparent in the time ahead those who have built their lives on the kingdom that cannot be shaken, and those who have built on the sand that the coming storms will wash away. Those who are growing in fear at the things coming upon the world have built their lives and hopes on this world. Those who are growing in the peace of the Lord, which is beyond human understanding, and will even seem ludicrous in the time to come, have built on the kingdom, and they will not be shaken.

NOTE FOR THE 2012 Edition

As stated, the 2008 edition was published just months before the crash of 2008. I am writing this on New Year's Eve 2011, and though the year has not yet begun, there are ominous signs that an even more devastating economic catastrophe is near. The Lord gave me this metaphor of the Titanic as a prophecy of economic disaster. Could it be upon us on this 25th anniversary of the discovery of the Titanic on the bottom of the sea?

If it is, or if it is delayed, we are hurtling fast toward the greatest economic debacle in history. Even so, the prepared prosper in every situation. Though our nation may be shaken to its foundation, it may be just what is needed to deliver us from the foolishness we have allowed for so long. This could be a reset, a jubilee, if we are prepared.

To be prepared, we first must be delivered from our own foolishness that Paul prophesied would come upon many in the last days where they only wanted "to have their ears tickled" or to hear sweet, happy things. To be people of the truth, we must be able to see the world as it is, not as we may want it to be. Just a couple of factors should alert us to the truth that we have allowed economic conditions which cannot possibly be sustained, and yet no one has had the courage to deal with it.

As the saying goes, "If you do not change your direction, you will end up where you are headed," and where we are headed is a major, worldwide economic meltdown. If it does not happen this year, it will likely be because the *government threw everything they could into keeping it from happening in an election year.*

Consider these basic factors: In just these last four years, the national debt of the U.S. grew more than it has from the time when George Washington was President until 2008. We are now asking for a new increase in our debt limit by over a trillion dollars every few months! As more are crying out that the country is being bankrupted, I have news for you—we have been bankrupt for a long time. No other organization on earth would be allowed to continue with the balance sheet of our U.S. Government.

*As I wrote in **The Harvest** (which was the full vision I had received in 1987), there will be a worldwide economic collapse that begins with an earthquake in Japan and is followed by others on our West Coast. In 2011, the terrible earthquake and resulting tsunami devastated a large portion of Japan. I am now expecting earthquakes, tsunamis, and volcanoes on the U.S. West Coast. Others have seen devastation along the New Madrid fault line in the center of the country. Others have seen similar catastrophes on the East Coast. We all see in part, and those who have seen these I have a high regard for. Even so, until they have* *happened, we can still appeal to God for mercy. He always prefers mercy over judgment, but there are conditions that must be met, which we see in II Chronicles 7:14:*

If My people, who are called by My name will humble themselves, and pray and seek My face, and turn from their wicked ways, then I will hear from heaven, and will forgive their sin and heal their land (NKJV).

We see here four conditions: 1) humility, 2) prayer, 3) seeking His face, and 4) repenting of wickedness. So how do we measure up to these now?

In some ways, we may measure up better than we think. As we see in the Lord's response to wicked King Ahab, it does not take much humility at all for the Lord to respond with mercy. Has there been enough? Has there been any? I think we should not take this for granted and seek to humble ourselves every way that we can.

Next is prayer. In this I think we are certainly better off. Some of the greatest prayer movements in history have arisen in our times, and many have become deeply burdened for the nations. Is it enough? The Lord knows, but

I think we should seek to excel in this more and more.

Next is seeking His face. This has been a rich and powerfully presented message to the church for decades now. Many have obeyed, and more are being captured by the necessity of His presence and close fellowship with Him. Is it enough? The Lord knows, but certainly there is nothing else we should be seeking in this world more than to abide in Him. However, as a nation, the U.S. has basically been running from God at an increasingly fast pace, seeking to remove even the mention of Him from our public places, schools, and even our conversation. The meltdown in the fabric of our society has followed the trajectory of this.

The last was to repent of our wicked ways. First, this wickedness must be God's definition of wickedness, which He is very clear about in the Scriptures. In this I don't think there is any doubt there has been a tragic and profound failure. The increase of wickedness has reached the exponential curve in the U.S. and Western society in general. It certainly seems that the salt has lost its savor, and the light is no longer shinning in the darkness. This is a primary reason why the Islamic world thinks that the perversion is so great in the West that the only remedy is to totally destroy Western civilization, and the U.S. in particular, because Hollywood is at the root of world spiritual and moral pollution. Of course, I don't agree with this remedy, but I do understand why those cultures and religious people that hold to a sense of decency and morality are increasingly outraged at the U.S. and the West for what is being spewed all over the earth from us.

Many kinds of judgment are in Scripture, only one of which is destruction, and only one of which is condemnation—the rest are all discipline from the Lord for those whom He loves. However, when discipline comes we must remember that it is a sign that God has not given up on us, but is calling us to repentance so that we might live.

WAR AND
GLORY

I was in a vision, standing on an island in the middle of a sea. Many different types of buildings were spread out in groups all around the island, which seemed to make up separate little cities. Within each of these little cities, the buildings seemed to clash with each other in color and architecture. There were very old ones next to very modern ones. This made them all seem unattractive and confused.

A war was going on between the occupants of many in the buildings, and many were already bombed out shells. The people who were still living in the buildings were starving and wounded. At first I thought that I had been caught in the middle of a terrible civil war. Then I realized that this was the church.

As I continued looking, I saw two dark spirits over the island. Together they were directing the battles and clashes between the buildings. One was named Jealousy, and the other one Fear. They congratulated each other every time one of the buildings suffered damage or people were killed or wounded. It seemed that no one who was involved in the fighting could see these spirits though they dominated the island.

As I kept looking, two even more powerful and frightening spirits were rising up over the sea. These became great storms. One was named Rage, and the other Lawlessness. They quickly started stirring up the sea and causing great waves to crash into the island. Soon these storms became so large that I felt they were going to do even more damage to the island than the war, and maybe even destroy the whole island. Even so, the war had the people in the buildings so occupied that it did not seem that anyone was aware of these growing storms.

I knew that the people in the city had to be warned about the storms. Then I saw several apparent watchmen trying to do this, but no one would listen to them. Those who could hear the watchmen only debated and argued about whether the watchmen should be trusted. This was remarkable because anyone who just looked up could see the storms for themselves, but no one would look up.

These wars had left so many people wounded that the hospitals were fast becoming the largest buildings on the island. I knew that these hospitals were movements or denominations that had given themselves to healing the wounded. The very small hospitals seemed to be respected, and the warring factions would not attack them. The ones that had grown larger were being attacked as the jealousy of the warring factions had them focus on the hospitals. They did this even though their own wounded were being cared for in them. As I watched, the attacks on these hospitals from the other buildings increased until they became some of the biggest battles.

Time passed swiftly before me like pages being turned in a book. The conflict went on and on. Soon everyone was wounded somewhere, but even those who were not badly wounded had the appearance of being either phantoms or grotesquely deformed from starvation and disease. Any time a building received a supply of food that would attract people, it would become a target. I could not comprehend how even a war could be so cruel *and yet this was the church!*

In the midst of the battle, men were still trying to add to their buildings or start new ones, but it was futile. Any time one building would start to rise a little higher than the others, it would become the main target of all of the other buildings close to it. When a new building was started, it would become the focus of unrelenting attacks by all of the others around it. My thought was that this entire island would soon be like the temple in Jerusalem after it was conquered by the Romans, and ultimately there would not be one stone left upon another.

I was then carried in the Spirit to a place where leaders who were conducting this war were gathered. All of them had the same word on their forehead: "Treachery." I was surprised that anyone would follow someone with that written on them, but they did. In fact, the most treacherous gained the most followers. I was reminded of II Corinthians 11:20, **"For you bear with anyone if he enslaves you, if he devours you, if he takes advantage of you, if he exalts himself, if he hits you in the face."** These were false shepherds and yet no one seemed to be confronting them, but rather the people would try to pick the strongest ones to follow.

The grief of this scene was nearly too much to bear. It was so obvious that if the effort and resources were put into building rather than what was going into fighting, there could be a city built with no equal, yet they had chosen the way of destruction instead.

The Remnant

As I continued to watch, I saw people who appeared as lights in almost every building. These lights refused to take part in the fighting, but spent their time trying to repair the buildings or nurse the wounded. Even though it was impossible to keep up with the damage or nurse the multitude of wounded, these courageous souls did not stop trying. I knew quickly that these were the true shepherds, but there were not many, and there were not many following them.

To work as hard and faithfully as these did in the circumstances made me feel that they were some of the greatest souls who had walked the earth. They were truly amazing in their character and endurance, and it was a tragedy that they did not seem to be recognized or followed by many for who they were.

These lights had the power to heal wounds, and that power was increasing as they worked. Those who were healed became lights just as they were. It was obvious that those who were committed to healing the wounded were now able to do more than the hospitals because of the ruthlessness of the attacks on the hospitals. Seeming to understand this too, the hospitals began to disperse their people as "healing teams." Soon these teams had spread out across the island and moved into many of the other buildings. It was as I watched this happen that, for the first time, I began to have hope that this war could actually be stopped by the healers because their effect was being so quickly felt.

I was then shown many small camps around the perimeter of the island. Some of these were involved in the war between the buildings and seemed intent on trying to destroy all of the buildings so they could bring the people to their camps. The leaders of these camps had the same word "Treachery" written on their foreheads. These small camps were movements that considered their main attractive characteristics to be that they were "not like" those who were in the buildings. It's true that in a way they were not like them because they had camps instead of buildings, but they were of the very same spirit and doing the same kind of damage to others.

Then I noticed that a few of these camps were not involved in the war. These were composed of those who almost all appeared to be lights. It was hard to understand why everyone could not see the difference in these, but a few could.

As I watched, these lights grew in authority, but it was a different authority than the healing powers that the others had. They had authority over events. They were praying to stop small battles and to keep small storms away, and it was happening as they prayed. Like the healing teams in the city, I began to feel that these too really could have an impact and change the terrible situation that this little island was now in. I felt that when these lights found and joined the healing teams in the city that they could truly become a formidable force for good. As one group stopped a battle, the other could go in and quickly heal all of the wounded. In this way their numbers would grow much faster.

I then noticed that the two large spirits over the city and the two over the storms took notice of these small camps where the lights were dwelling. They quickly became very agitated by them since it was obvious that they were intimidated by these small groups. These camps were growing in authority so fast that they were soon close to having the authority to stop even the big battles and big storms, which was obviously the source of agitation for these large spirits.

As I was looking at the storms, I noticed multitudes of boats and ships all around the island. They were waiting to enter the city as soon as the fighting stopped. Many of these boats were full of refugees from other wars, and many were wounded. There were also ships bearing kings and presidents, and others that carried those who appeared wealthy and prosperous. These ships were all aware of and afraid of the storms and wanted to make it into the safety of the ports, but they could not enter them because of the fighting. Their groans and screams became so loud I was surprised that no one on the island could hear them. It did not even seem that anyone was aware of these ships wanting to come in.

The Lord Comes to Build His House

Then I saw the Lord standing and watching. He was so brilliant that I wondered why I had not seen Him before or why everyone in the city did not see Him. I approached some people to point them to the Lord, but I then looked into their eyes and saw that they were so bloodshot I was surprised they could see anything.

I then wondered why the Lord did not stop the fighting. He seemed content to just watch. As if He had understood my thoughts, He turned and said to me, *"This is My church. These were the houses men tried to build for Me. I knocked on the door of each one, but they would not open to Me. I would have brought peace. I will only dwell in the city of peace."*

Then He turned and indicated to the people in the ships, saying: *"If I allowed all of these people to come to the city now they would just be used in the war. When their cries become louder than the war, I will build a place for them."*

Then He looked at me with great earnestness and said, *"I allowed this to happen so that it would never happen again!"* It is hard to convey the power I felt when the Lord said this, but it imparted to me a deep understanding that He allowed this conflict to continue out of profound wisdom. He then said, *"Until you understand this wisdom, you cannot understand what I am about to do."*

When the cries of those in the boats became louder than the conflict in the city, the Lord gave a command and the sea was released. Great tidal waves arose and began to sweep across the island until they covered the buildings. The spirits that were storms joined the spirits over the island, and they all grew to almost double their previous size. Then the island completely disappeared under the darkness of the spirits and the raging sea.

The Lord did not move as this was happening. I knew that my only protection was to stand as close to Him as possible. I could not see anything but Him during this great storm. As I looked at His face, I could see both pain and resolve.

Slowly, the storms died down and the tides receded. Though it did not seem that anyone could have survived, those who were the lights in the buildings began to emerge. They remained standing where the buildings had once been. Then the Lord, who had been on the edge of the island, moved to the center and said, *"Now I will build My house."*

All of those who were lights started to see the Lord and began turning toward Him. As they turned, they became even brighter, and each group was changed into a living pillar right where they stood. Soon it became obvious that these pillars were the framework of a building which would cover almost the entire island.

The pillars were different colors, shapes, and sizes. It was hard to understand how all of these being so different would work as a single framework. However, the Lord seemed very pleased with each one, and soon they all did start to fit together.

Then the ships and boats, which had been offshore, all started landing on the island. There were multitudes of people. Each ship or boat was from a different country, culture, or a race of people. Soon I began to think that even as large as the building was, there were too many people for it. Then the Lord looked at me and said sternly, *"We will build as many rooms as we need—no one will be turned away."*

This was said so sternly that I resolved to never again consider that turning people away was an option. I also pondered how the biggest problem before was how to get people to come to the buildings. Now the big problem was what to do with all of the people.

The Cemetery

When each ship arrived, the people on it were led straight to the Lord. He looked into the eyes of each one and said, *"If you trust Me you will die for Me."* When each one said, "I will die for You," the Lord immediately thrust His sword right through their hearts. This caused very real pain in each one. To those who tried to avoid the sword, it was obviously even more painful. To those who relaxed, it did not seem to hurt as much.

These were then taken to a cemetery with the word, "Obscurity" over the gate. I followed them to see what was done with them. Those who had been thrust through the heart were checked to see that they were really dead before they were buried. Some clung to life for a long time and were laid off to one side. Then, those who were buried quickly began to arise as lights just like those who had survived the storm. I noticed that they were not staying in their tombs the same length of time. Some of these arose before those who were clinging to life were even buried.

When I first looked at this cemetery, it looked like a dreadful place. I did not think it fit with what had now become such a beautiful island. As I left the cemetery, I turned to look back at it, and it was more than beautiful—it was glorious! I could not figure out what was different, when one of the workers said to me knowingly, "The cemetery has not changed—you have."

I then looked at the building and it was even more wonderful than I had remembered. I looked over the entire island that I could see and felt the same thing—it had all become much more beautiful. I remembered the Scripture, **"Precious in the sight of the Lord is the death of His godly ones" (Psalm 116:15).** The worker, who was still looking at me, then said, "You have not died yet but were changed just by being close to those who have. When you die, you will see even more glory." Those who were emerging as lights from the cemetery were each being led to their own place in the building. That place would have their name on it. Some joined the walls, others joined the pillars, and some became windows or doors. They remained people even after they became a part of the building. The way they fit together was too remarkable to have been the result of any kind of human engineering.

The Test

I returned to the Lord's side. Standing in His presence was so wonderful I could not imagine why anyone would not be willing to die for Him. Even so, many of the people coming from the ships did refuse. These would all back away from Him at the request. Many of these went back to the ships, some of which started back out to sea, and some of which remained in the harbor.

A few of the people who refused to die stayed on the island and were allowed to walk about freely, even enter the house of the Lord. They seemed to love and bask in the glory of it all. Many of these began to shine with a glory too, but they never had the glory within themselves—they only reflected what was coming from the others.

As I was thinking that it was not right for these to be allowed to stay, the Lord said to me, *"My patience will win many of these, but even those that never give Me their lives, I love, and am pleased to let them enjoy My goodness. Never turn away those who love My glory."* These really did enjoy the house and enjoyed the presence of the Lord that radiated from the house. Even so, they seemed timid and retreated when the Lord Himself came close to them.

I then watched as those who had refused to die for the Lord began to act as if His house was their own and had been built for them. I wanted to be angry at their presumption, but I could not feel anger even though I wanted to. I then understood that it was because I was standing so close to the Lord that I could not get mad. This forced me to make the decision to stay close to Him or move away so that I could be angry.

I was surprised that this was a difficult decision, that I would even consider wanting to move away from the Lord, but it was. Out of fear at what was arising within me, I stepped closer to the Lord. He immediately reached out and grabbed me as if I were about to fall off of a cliff. As I looked behind me, I was astonished to find that I had been on the very edge of one, and had I taken that one step away from Him to feel the anger, I would have stepped off of it. He then said to me, *"In this house I can tolerate presumption more than that anger. That anger would start the war again."*

As I was still disconcerted by how close I had come to falling off of the cliff, I began to be over-whelmed with the knowledge that I had not yet made the decision to die for Him either. I, too, had been presumptuously feeling possessive of both the house *and* the Lord, and I was in fact just like the others who were walking around feeling possessive of these and had not given my life to Him. "I am the same hypocrite that I despised in others," I thought. As I saw this great evil in my own heart, I was so appalled that I begged the Lord to destroy my evil heart with His sword. He did not hesitate.

Resurrection Life

When the Lord pierced my heart, I was surprised to feel so little pain when it seemed to have been so hard on others. He then said to me as I was fading out of consciousness, *"Those who request death die easier."* I remembered His statement in Matthew 21:44: **"And he who falls on this stone will be broken to pieces; but on whoever it falls, it will scatter him like dust."**

I did not remember being carried to the cemetery, but just as if no time at all had passed, I was emerging from it again. Now the glory of every thing I saw was unspeakable. I looked at a rock and loved it. I looked at the trees, the sky, and the clouds, and could not believe how wonderful they were. A sparrow seemed more glorious than any bird I had ever seen. I stood wondering at the great treasure that this little bird was and why I had not appreciated them like this before.

I then looked at the presumptuous people. Not only did I feel no temptation to be angry with them, I loved them so much I felt that it would be worth it to die again for each one. I began to think about how blessed I was to be able to meet them and be with them—there was so much to know and learn from each one.

"People really are great treasures," I heard a familiar voice say. *"Now you know why I would have gone to the cross even for just one."* I wanted all of these people to stay on the island now and could not even comprehend how I was ever tempted to be angry at them—they were much greater treasures than the sparrow! "What a joy it is going to be to serve them," I thought.

Then, as the Lord stood next to me, I turned to look at Him. Though I did not think it was possible, He was much more glorious than before, and yet I was able to bear it. He said, *"This is why the death of My people is so precious to Me. Those who seek to save their lives always lose them, but those who lose their lives for My sake find true life. Now you know true life because you know love."*

"I would have gone to the cross for just one of these, and in a sense I do for each one. My death still works through My people so that My resurrection life can also work through them. Someone goes to the cross, lays down their life in some way, for the rebirth

of every soul. It is in this way, when such a price is paid, that people become treasures to one another. The value of anything is in what someone is willing to pay for it. What will you pay for these? Will you die daily that they might live?"

I realized that just shortly before I had wanted to drive these very people from the place, and now I really did feel that it would be worth it to die again for each one. I knew then that death truly is the path to life because it is the path to love. When you feel this way, death did not even seem to be a great price to pay. The whole earth and all of its treasure did not seem worth a single one of these souls.

"You now have one job," the Lord continued. *"That is to love. Love causes pain. You must lay down your life for those you love. The pain that you suffer is what you are paying for souls. The pain that you suffer in this way is accumulating for you an eternal treasure."*

I then looked at the house and all of those who composed it. Everything and everyone that I looked at seemed to stir up this great feeling of love that was more wonderful than anything I had ever felt before. I wanted to go look at or talk to each one, but I did not want to leave the Lord's side whose presence was even more wonderful. Knowing my thoughts, He said, *"You need never fear leaving My side, because I have made My abode in you, and I will be with you everywhere that you go."*

As I watched the presumptuous people, they were enjoying all of the blessings and even thought of themselves as the reason for them. However, they were not even a part of what was being built. Having just been one of them I also knew how shallow their enjoyment was compared to what it could be. As I continued watching these people, they gradually became thinner in substance until they were just like the phantoms I had seen in the city that had been destroyed. They were really empty shells who only had life because they were close to those who were so rich in it. Before I would have scorned and held these people in contempt. I now felt great compassion for them and I wanted to help them in any way I could. I was marveling almost as much in the change in me as I was in the great building that was going up and the great glories that now seemed to be everywhere. Love gave me eyes to see.

No Limits

Then I looked at how the building kept getting higher. The higher it went, the more glory it exuded and the farther it could be seen. This resulted in even more ships and people coming through the storms, which were still raging out to sea, but now seemed unable to affect the island.

As I wondered how high the building could go, the Lord turned to me again, and as if He were answering my thoughts said, *"There is no limit to how high we can build this because I am the foundation and love is the cement. I am not limited, and neither is love."*

This caused me to look at the cement, which was transparent but radiated power. I wondered how I had not noticed this before because it was now so obvious and captivating. I then started pondering how I seemed blind to even the greatest wonders of this building until the Lord directed my attention to them. This caused me to turn back to the Lord and watch everything that He gave His attention to. I had eyes to see, but they were still dependent on Him.

The Lord then began looking at the people who now composed the building. As I looked at them again, I saw that they were in fact *more* than people—they were the "new creation" who had transcended this creation. They had bridged the gap between the physical and spiritual realms, and yet were clearly a part of both. They were supernatural beings. This did not mean that they were not natural, but rather they were far more natural than anything "natural" I had ever seen. They were more real than anything I had ever considered "real." They made everything else seem like a shadow, and this sense increased as they continued to change.

Soon the glory that was coming from them could be both seen and felt. The feeling was not like a touch but like an emotion. As I walked close enough to this glory, it made me feel so good that the only way I can describe it is like a wonderful intoxication. However, it was not an intoxication that clouded the mind but rather illuminated and focused it. I felt somehow ennobled, not with pride, but with a powerful sense of destiny. I also felt a security, as if I were in complete harmony with the ground, the air, and especially the Lord and His house. This feeling was so good that I never wanted to move again.

With the addition of each new boatload of people, the transformation of those already a part of the building would continue, and the glory of the whole building would increase and expand. This made everyone in the building rejoice with the coming of each new group of people.

Sharing the Glory

When those who came from the cemetery took their places in the building, those who were already a part tried to give the new ones their own glory. As they did this, the glory radiating from the Lord would increase, and He would give those who had given away their own glory even more. Those who were the most devoted to this sharing would be the ones used to start the next level of the house, which kept going higher and higher.

I thought about how opposite this was from the jealousy which had before prevailed in the city. I then tried to ponder the jealousy to understand it more, but it was almost impossible to do. Because I could no longer feel jealousy, I had a difficult time even understanding what it was—it seemed as unreal as if it had only existed in bad dreams. The joy of sharing was so great that not to do it now seemed incomprehensible. The more the glory was shared, the more one received to share.

This joy of sharing was so great that I knew all of us would be spending eternity just seeking others with whom to share the glory. I had a sense of knowing that the Lord would be creating many new worlds just for us to have new places to share His glory. I then knew that this was why He had created the universe with such diversity and why He created it to continually expand. Our capacity to experience His glory would be forever expanding just like the universe. Those who touched His glory were touched by a love that had to share the glory, which caused them to expand. He had given us the universe to share His glory with. He had set in motion a glorious chain reaction of glory that would never stop! There were no limits on time or space, and we would need every bit of it!

The Storms Return

Then suddenly my attention was turned toward the storms. I had been so caught up in the glory of this house that I had not realized that they had continued to grow out in the sea. To my shock they had grown larger and faster than the house of the Lord and were now coming toward the island.

Before anything could be done, great waves covered the island. The building disappeared from my view even though I was still very close to it. The fury of this storm was beyond any earthly storm I had ever known. Even so, I felt no fear at all. I knew that it was because I had already died to this world, and now I had a life that could never be taken from me.

As wonderful as the island had become, I was just as happy to die physically so I would be free to carry the glory of the Lord to the rest of the universe that had so captured my attention. It really would have been hard to choose to stay or go, so I just rested and waited to see whether I would die again or not. Death was no longer fearful at all, but rather inviting, like a door to another great adventure or experience.

Gradually, the storms abated and the building then reemerged. Both the building and the island were much smaller, but were even more glorious. Then I noticed that the storms were just offshore and returning. This happened several times. Each time the building would emerge it would be smaller but more glorious. Each time that this happened the storms were also much smaller—they were wearing themselves out on the island.

Soon the storms could only generate small waves that were no threat to do any real damage.

The glory of the house was now beyond any human description. Then the clouds dissipated altogether into the most beautiful sky I had ever seen on the earth. It was obvious now that heaven had penetrated the realm of earth.

As I gazed into the sky, I began to realize that it was filled with the glory that was being emitted from the house. As I looked at the house, I was amazed that there was no damage from the storm, though it was much smaller. Even so, the glory now coming from the house was much greater than before and was reflected by everything. I felt that it was so great it must already be extending far beyond the earth into the heavens.

Then the vision changed, and I was alone with the Lord. All of the great feelings were gone—even the love. He looked at me earnestly and said, *"The war is almost over. It is time to prepare for the storms. Tell My people that no one with his brother's blood on his hands will be used to build My house."*

I was trying hard to listen to these words in order to heed them, while still thinking about the great love I had felt, but no longer did. He then said, *"This was a dream, but it is real. You have known everything that I have shown you in this dream. You have experienced it in your heart. Now believe with your heart and My love will be real to you again. This is your quest—to know My love."*

THE NEXT WAVE IS UPON US

On May 11, 1992 I saw a surfer floating on a short surfboard, gazing at the beach, lazily drifting and dreaming of the big wave. I knew this surfer was the body of Christ, the church. While this surfer was drifting, the very wave he was dreaming about was getting closer and closer, but he did not know it. I knew that unless he woke up and looked around very fast, it would come crashing down on top of him. I also knew that his board was too short for the huge wave that was coming.

It was obvious that because of his sleepy state, the very wave this surfer dreamed about placed him in serious jeopardy because he was not ready for it as it approached. By the time he did hear the sound of the wave and turned to look, it was too late. What had been the desire of his heart became a terror. The wave turned the surfer over and over, smashing him into the bottom several times and breaking his board. I feared for his life but he survived, though with many cuts, bruises, and a few broken bones.

I watched the surfer lying on the beach in great pain. Soon the terror of possibly dying passed and a deep wisdom replaced it. He gazed back out over the sea. Even though he was so broken and hurt that he could hardly move, an awesome resolve came over him. I knew he would be back to ride the waves again.

I then saw this surfer in a hospital with a room that looked out over the ocean. He was still gazing at the sea, but I knew that instead of dreaming, he was now planning. I then saw him standing on the beach, not only healed but far more muscular than he had been before. Next to him stood the largest surfboard I have ever seen.

Even though the sea was calm, he knew that the biggest wave of all was already in motion beyond the horizon. He was ready, and believed he could ride the wave, but fears were rising up in him. If he did not quickly dismiss them and get moving, he would not be able to paddle out far enough in time to catch it, but instead would again be in great jeopardy from the wave.

Many other surfers also looked like professional bodybuilders and were standing all over the beach. These all had the short boards and were bodybuilders who really did not seem interested in the waves at all, but just in showing off their bodies, which actually looked unnatural, even grotesque. Their large, bulging muscles were not really as strong as the real surfer's, whose muscles seemed more natural and for strength, not just show.

Interpretation

In the previous great awakenings or revivals in church history, there have been very few who were anticipating the move of the Holy Spirit. In almost every great awakening or revival, the existing churches and ministries were damaged by the new move simply because they were not ready for it. Some of these have had to actually resist the revival just to survive.

In contrast, today there seems to be an almost universal expectation of impending revival, but there has been very little actually done to prepare for it. Even though we may know it is coming, we have been spending more time dreaming about it than preparing for it. The wave of the Holy Spirit that is coming is bigger than we have dreamed, but because we are dreaming more than preparing, we are in jeopardy from the very wave we have been hoping to see.

The first surfboard was far too short and obviously inadequate for even a good size wave, much less the big one that came. This speaks of the inadequacy of the current vehicles, outreaches, and ministries of the church. I felt that even if the surfer had seen the wave in time he could not have ridden it—he would have either had to quickly paddle to the beach or out beyond where the wave was going to break and just watch it go by.

Like this surfer, the present church is in danger of getting nothing more than a good beating and a good lesson out of the impending move of the Holy Spirit. Even though the church has been hearing from the Lord about the impending harvest, few have not been acting on His words and actually taken practical steps to be ready for what is coming. The pounding we are likely to take from the next wave will bring wisdom though, and resolve to be ready for the next one, including having the proper vehicle for riding it. The time we spend recovering from the injuries of the impending wave must be spent in planning for the next one. Then our plans must be turned into action.

To ride the wave that is coming we will also need to be much stronger than we are now. Strength comes from *exercising*. When the surfer returned to the beach, he had the physique of a bodybuilder, but one who had built himself up for strength, not just show. Every muscle seemed perfectly formed and powerful.

The body of Christ must likewise be built up. Every muscle and every limb and every individual part of the body must be properly exercised and brought to full strength. For decades, we have been preaching on Ephesians 4 concerning the equipping of the saints for the work of service, but it is now time that we start doing it. This must not be done for show either, to just exhibit our beautiful body. We must do it with a focused attention on being ready for the next move of the Holy Spirit.

The Ephesians 4 emphasis of equipping the saints will again become fashionable. Many will become involved in this "spiritual bodybuilding" just for show. These will in truth be devoted more to impressing each other than preparing for the next move of the Spirit. They will not really have the proper equipment for or even be aware of what is going on in the sea (mass humanity). Those who build their congregations for show will actually look grotesque and will not have the proper skills for riding the wave of the Spirit or even be in the water when it comes.

Even though this surfer was properly prepared and had a proper board for riding the next wave, the enemy used the negative experience of the previous wave to hit him with a fear that could hinder him from accomplishing all that he had prepared for. All of our preparation and work will come to nothing if we are not utterly committed to getting back in the water and walking by faith, not by fear. To catch the wave we must:

1. Be adequately trained and in shape.

2. Have the proper board (vehicle or ministry).

3. Be properly positioned (having discerned where the wave is going to break and getting there).

4. Be watching so that we can, at the proper time, start paddling with the wave.

5. Be ready to act without hesitation when the wave breaks.

The church has been in the initial stages of a great worldwide revival that will ultimately result in the harvest that is the end of the age. As we see in Matthew 13:30, the harvest begins with the tares. Many of the exposés of evildoing and sin within the church have actually been a work of the Holy Spirit to prepare the church for the ingathering, which is soon to begin.

Every time the Lord has shown me the coming harvest, He has shown it to me in two great waves. More than two waves may be coming, but I know there will be at least two. The first one will be so great that almost everyone will believe that it is in fact the great harvest that is the end of the age, but there is another wave coming after it that will be much greater. The millions of new believers who will come on the next wave are all called to be laborers in the second one. These people must be properly equipped and prepared for the greater wave.

The first wave of revival that is coming on the church will be a blessing only to the churches that have been using their time wisely and have been truly equipping the saints to do the work of the service. This wave will actually be judgment to every ministry that has not been properly equipping their people or who have spent more time dreaming than preparing.

CATCHING THE NEXT WAVE

A great spiritual advance is now gaining momentum throughout the body of Christ. It has the potential to be as sweeping in its scope and impact as the greatest movements in church history. How can we discern it accurately and position ourselves properly to be a part of it?

Moves of the Holy Spirit are often compared to waves because their characteristics are common. If the Holy Spirit moves in waves, how do we catch them so as to be carried in the direction that He is going? Four basic steps a surfer uses can give us significant insight into what we must do to catch the waves of the Holy Spirit. If a surfer is going to catch a wave, he must first discern where it is going to break. Second, he must position himself properly at that point. Third, he must begin to move in the direction that the wave is going. Then he must not hesitate when it breaks, or it will just pass him by.

Looking Back to Look Ahead

Many are discerning enough to know that the Holy Spirit is moving again but are doing very little to position themselves properly to be a part of it. Every move of God is built upon the foundation of the previous moves. If we are going to discern where the next move of God is going to break, we need to discern the nature and pattern of the previous ones.

There is a spiritual "continuation principle" that we must understand, and submit to, if we are going to be a part of a move of the Holy Spirit. That is why Jesus submitted Himself to John's baptism. To "fulfill all righteousness," even the Lord had to properly honor those who had gone before Him and prepared His way. Jesus was asked by the chief priests and elders:

> **"By what authority are You doing these things, and who gave You this authority?"**
>
> **And Jesus answered and said to them, "I will ask you one thing too, which if you tell Me, I will also tell you by what authority I do these things.**
>
> **"The baptism of John was from what source, from heaven or from men?"** (see Matthew 21:23-25).

The Lord's response to their question was not an attempt to deflect their question—the answer to His question was the answer to their question. Jesus had credentials. John was there as the representative of the "old order" sent to declare that Jesus was in fact the one whom all of the prophets and wise men from the beginning had been speaking of.

Honor With Righteous Judgment

If we arrogantly point to previous movements as "the old order," and declare ourselves to be of "the new order," or just have the arrogance that we think we know all that we need to and can not learn from those who have gone before us, we have almost certainly disqualified ourselves from being a part of the new order. It will be those who view the previous movements with the honor they deserve, immersing themselves in their message and teachings, who will be qualified to receive the next level of authority. For any new movement to abide long on the earth, it must honor its spiritual fathers and mothers.

James gave an interesting exhortation concerning treatment of the Law, which was the "movement" that preceded Christianity:

Do not speak against one another, brethren. He who speaks against a brother,

127

or judges his brother, speaks against the law, and judges the law; but if you judge the law, you are not a doer of the law, but a judge of it.

There is only one Lawgiver and Judge, the One who is able to save and to destroy; but who are you who judge your neighbor?

Do not complain, brethren, against one another, that you yourselves may not be judged; behold, the Judge is standing right at the door (James 4:11-12; 5:9).

When we judge in such a way that we are criticizing, we are condemning ourselves to the opposition of God, who **"resists the proud, but gives grace to the humble" (see James 4:6 NKJV).** Criticism is one of the highest forms of pride. When we criticize others we are by that declaring ourselves to be superior to them. This may be true, but if we are better than others, it is only because of God's grace. To become proud of our own standing is to depart from the very foundation upon which we are standing—God's grace.

However, there is a "righteous judgment" that we must have. We are foolish if we do not try to learn from the mistakes of the previous movements. Even so, we must be careful how we view them, not as condemning our spiritual parents, but seeing where the potential for the same faults exist within us so that we can seek the grace to stand in those areas.

The failure to properly understand righteous and unrighteous judgment is the reason for many of the greatest failures of the church in history and is one of the most important issues facing the church today. Until we understand them and walk by that understanding, we will continue to stumble over a deadly stumbling block.

The church both historically and presently has been prone to use unrighteous judgment while utterly neglecting the righteous judgment. Many watchdog ministries and Christian journalists have stumbled while sincerely trying to help fill a tragic void in church government. They fall because they have moved into a realm of authority to which they have not been appointed. Meanwhile, the elders neglect the authority which they have been given to exercise. Every new movement will continue to fall short of its potential until this important issue is resolved.

Paddling With the Wave

Some are discerning where the next wave is going to break and are positioning themselves properly but are hesitant about moving until the wave is upon them. These are in as much danger of missing the wave as those who have not positioned themselves at all. The most important thing that we can do to be moving with the wave when it comes is to obey and implement that which was imparted to the church through the last move.

A major source of the hesitancy that causes many to miss the moves of the Holy Spirit is a religious spirit rooted in human idealism that will not move until something is "totally God." The Lord does not do anything without man. A farmer was once being congratulated by a minister on the precision and lushness of his cornfield, remarking that he could not have done that without God. "I agree," said the farmer, "But He could not do it without me either. You should see the field I let Him grow all by Himself!"

There is an important point to this story. God commissioned man to "cultivate the garden." Man's work on earth is not unnatural, but man is a part of the nature of the world which God created. Likewise, He has commissioned fallible men to do the work of the ministry. We must keep in mind that the Holy Spirit is "the Helper," not "the Doer." Even the greatest man of God is an earthen vessel, imperfect and frail, and as James explained, **"for we all stumble in many ways" (see James 3:2).** Our work will never be perfect, but it can be acceptable to God. If He had wanted it perfect, He would have stayed here to do it all Himself.

The Lord left the church in the hands of men who appeared to be quite unstable and prone to mistakes, and they did make mistakes. We all must grow in grace and wisdom. If we had to wait until we were perfect to minister, no one would ever be qualified. Perfectionists who require unrealistic standards are like the Pharisees who would not enter the kingdom themselves and tried to hinder everyone else from entering as well. Every true move of God has begun with a considerable amount of humanity mixed in at first. There will even be tares mixed in with the wheat that the enemy plants. If you are going to wait until all of the tares are removed before you give yourself to the cultivating, you will miss everything.

Wait for the Big One

There is another factor that is required if we want to catch the biggest wave—we must resist catching the smaller ones. There are patterns to incoming waves which experienced surfers learn to recognize. Patience is required if they are going to ride the biggest and best wave. Likewise, in the Spirit there are many movements to which we can give ourselves, and many projects we can become involved in, but are they what we have been called to? How many of these are only working to displace us from our position when the big one comes?

This is not to discourage anyone from devotion to service and ministry. Indeed, the only way we will be in shape and skilled enough to catch the big wave is by practicing on the smaller ones. However, when we have been adequately prepared, and we know that the big one is coming, we must let the smaller ones go by. Many who miss the great moves of God do so because they are already too busy.

The Opposition

Each wave will try to make it as far up the beach as it can. Then the wave recedes, undercutting the next wave, making it break sooner than it would otherwise. Seldom have those who were a part of one move of God gone on to be a part of the next move. Usually those of a previous move are retreating as the next wave advances, creating a clash that hinders the next incoming wave. For every incoming wave, some of its greatest opposition will be from the previous waves that are retreating.

Throughout church history, those who were a part of one move of God have tried to resist and undercut those of the next move. However, even though this has continually been our history, it does not have to be our future. Before the end, there will be a movement that will capture the hearts of those in the previous movements so that they will join the advance rather than continue the retreat. When this happens, the church will begin a spiritual advance that will not be stopped until the end of the age.

Looking at some of the historic factors that have caused others to retreat can help us discern these stumbling blocks. The first dangerous delusion is for us to think that we would never oppose a true move of God. It has happened to some of the greatest men of God in history. The arrogance that it cannot happen to us can be the very thing that disqualifies us from God's grace, which He only gives to the humble (see James 4:6).

Andrew Murray is a good example of how even a great man of God, with a passion for seeing revival come to the church, can fail to recognize the very revival that he had spent his entire life praying for. The cause for this tragic failure was simple. The revival that he hoped for, and even prophesied, did not come in the form that he was expecting. Though he earnestly desired to see the release of spiritual gifts within the church again, he was offended by the package they arrived in. He and his followers may have been offended that it did not come through them. Regardless, he ended up missing what he had spent his life prophesying and praying for.

Sadly, most new movements are led by relatively immature leaders. This is because the mature leaders have become "old wineskins," too inflexible to receive the new wine. Spiritual movements must be led by the Spirit who requires flexibility and openness. Usually the only ones He can find that are flexible enough are the immature, because they have not yet become inflexible with preconceived ideas. Immature leaders are therefore more prone to be dependent on the Holy Spirit than on their experience, allowing Him to direct as He chooses. This is probably why the Lord chose such unlikely and "unqualified" men as the foundational leaders of His church. They were so unqualified that they were desperately dependent upon His grace and guidance.

True Faith

Rarely does a spiritual leader arise with great experience and wisdom combined with a sensitive dependency upon the Holy Spirit. However, such leadership is certainly preferable to that of the immature. The immature do allow the Holy Spirit to lead, which is the highest form of wisdom, but they often allow other influences to gain entry because of their lack of experience. It is for this reason that the Lord always seems to give opportunity to leaders of previous movements to lead the next move. The greatest leaders will know how to let the Holy Spirit lead, while having the experience and discernment to keep the movement out of the hands of the lawless or legalistic.

Two good biblical examples of those with maturity and experience combined with flexibility and dependency on the Holy Spirit are Joshua and Caleb. Such will also be required for the movement that leads the church across her Jordan River into the battle for her Promised Land. Not only were Joshua and Caleb men of great faith in the Lord, but their faith was not diluted by many years of wandering in the wilderness with a faithless people.

Such faith could only be the result of two great spiritual factors. First, true faith is not encouraged or discouraged by the condition of the people, because it is not faith in people but in God. Second, true faith is not limited by time but always views from the perspective of eternity. That is why the great men of faith in Scripture were content to view the fulfillment of the promises prophetically without having to receive them in their own time.

It is most difficult to grow in wisdom, experience, and age compared to other men while remaining humble. This is because of our tendency to judge ourselves by our comparison to other men, rather than to the only true Standard—Christ Jesus. Measuring ourselves by other men or our church by other churches is one of the most deadly stumbling blocks to spiritual leaders. As Paul said, **"but when**

they measure themselves by themselves, and compare themselves with themselves, they are without understanding" (see II Corinthians 10:12).

True faith does not look at men and it does not look at the temporary. Some of the Lord's most anointed messages caused the crowds to wither away. How many of us would be willing to preach a sermon that we knew would cause most of our congregation to leave us? How many of us love the approval of God more than men to be willing to do this?

The truly wise will not be overly encouraged when men gather around them or discouraged when they depart. If we receive our encouragement from men, it only proves that we have received our authority from men. If we receive our authority from above, then no man can take it away, and we will not be overly concerned by either the approval or disapproval of men. That is why when men came to make Jesus king, He fled to the mountains. If men make you king, then men will also rule you, regardless of what title you are given.

Jesus unquestionably had the greatest compassion for the human condition. However, He never responded to human need—He only did what He saw the Father doing. The Lord did not just call us to do good works in His name but to do the work that He called us to do. One of the greatest stumbling blocks to walking in true ministry is the tendency to take the people's yokes instead of the Lord's yoke. The people's yokes will have us busy doing many things that appear good and fruitful, but they will not have us doing the Lord's will.

How many of us could, like Philip, begin a revival that stirs an entire city, then give that work into the hands of others so that we can go witness to just one man? The reason Philip could be entrusted with such authority and power to stir a city was because of his obedience. If he were just focused on men, or the temporary, he would never have left Samaria. However, it is probable that the fruit of that one Ethiopian eunuch's conversion was much greater than the revival in Samaria. Centuries later, missionaries were astonished to find that when they arrived in Ethiopia there were so many Christians already there. This fruit had been hidden to men, and probably even to Philip, but it was certainly credited to his account.

Obedience, Not Sacrifice

It is obedience, not sacrifice, which will keep us in the will of God. I do not think that I have ever met a true Christian who did not long to be in the center of the activity of God. However, we must know that not all good activity is God's activity. We must also understand that it is not possible for all of us to be a part of everything that He is doing. The most important issue is not just catching the "big wave," but catching the one that He wants us to catch, while cheering on those who may be catching the bigger ones and the smaller ones, if they are in God's will.

As we keep our vision on the goal of seeing the water move as far up the beach as possible, and holding all of the ground that we can take, we will be in a better position to move forward with the next wave rather than retreating and undercutting it. It does not matter who leads a wave as long as *the* Leader gets the glory. To have any other attitude is to be as deluded as the donkey's colt that Jesus rode into Jerusalem on, if he thought that all of the commotion and adoration was for him instead of the One riding on his back.

Jon Amos Comenius stated that "Nature is God's second book." The Apostle Paul affirmed this in the first chapter of Romans. One of the great leadership lessons in nature is found with migrating waterfowl such as geese and ducks. They fly in "V" formations because the lead bird creates a draft that makes the flying easier for those who follow closely behind him. However, since the lead bird cutting through the air is doing the most work, he will only stay on the point for a period of time, and then he will drop back to the end of the formation and rest, and the next one moves up to lead for awhile. This rotation allows the birds to share the burden of leadership, and all benefit from the draft when others are leading. If a bird refused to give up his leadership position at the proper time, he would begin to slow down the whole flock. Those who give up their position at the proper time will have a chance to rest while following in the wake of others, enabling them to again assume the point at another time.

Seldom in church history has any leader been on the cutting edge for more than a few years. However, it is a most difficult thing for a leader to give up leadership. For those who refused to do this, there is a clear demarcation point in their lives when they stopped going forward and started attacking those who did.

Flying geese do not have as their goal being the point bird, but rather getting to the destination. Whenever our own position becomes a goal in itself, we will become more of a hindrance to the advancement of the church than a leader of it. One can have great influence and control other people long after he has lost the true anointing for spiritual leadership. King Saul is one of the more obvious biblical examples of this principle.

Saul's counterpart, King David, was not just an extraordinary leader in his own time, but he had the wisdom to realize the limits of his authority. When he understood that it was not his destiny to build the temple, he began gathering materials to pass on to his heir in order to make his job easier. The greatest leaders not only know how far to go themselves—they know how to prepare for the next generation and when to pass the scepter.

Summary

Leadership is a valuable gift. The desire to be on the cutting edge of what God is doing, to be in the middle of the action, is usually evidence of our love for the Lord and our desire to a part of what He is doing. However, if our motives are not right, it can also be one of our most prideful and disobedient pursuits. It is right to want to push back the darkness, to help the body of Christ climb to higher ground, but are we doing this for the Lord's glory or for our own? If we are not doing it for ourselves, we should be just as glad to prepare others to do it and to cheer them on. Is that not what the great cloud of witnesses is doing right now for us?

Being on the cutting edge, or being with a group that is, is not the most important goal in life. When we stand before the throne of God on that great Judgment Day, He is not going to count how many cutting edge movements we were a part of. We are going to be judged by our obedience, by how much we have grown in love, and by how much of His likeness we bear. In Christ it is true that the greatest leaders are the greatest followers. The more closely we follow Him, the more of His glory we will behold, and the more like Him we will become.

To fulfill all righteousness and to walk in the spiritual authority to which we have been called requires that we properly honor those who have gone before us and have made our way easier. It is also true that we must be willing to prepare the way for those who will carry the work further. We must all be willing to let go when the time is right. It was David's willingness to pass on to the next generation the greatest desire of his own heart that enabled God to entrust him with the extraordinary leadership for his own generation.

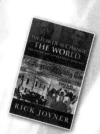